1981

CHILD ABUSE

p 101

p. 100

p. 30

95134

CHILD ABUSE

A Crying Shame

Shirley O'Brien

Brigham Young University Press

Library of Congress Cataloging in Publication Data

O'Brien, Shirley, 1938–
 Child abuse, a crying shame.

 Bibliography: p. 186
 1. Child abuse—United States.   2. Child molesting—
United States.   3. Child abuse—Services—United States.
4. Child abuse—United States—Prevention.   I. Title.
HV741.027   362.7'044   80-23708
ISBN 0-8425-1829-0

Library of Congress Catalog Number: 80-23708
International Standard Book Number: 0-8425-1829-0
Brigham Young University Press, Provo, Utah 84602
© 1980 Brigham Young University Press. All rights reserved
Printed in the United States of America
80 46911

Contents

Introduction

Child abuse and neglect must be stopped. It is an ugly blight on our record as caring human beings moving through the twentieth century. You might agree, but you might also say you're glad it's someone else's problem, not yours. If so, you are not alone in your thinking. Many people feel the same way. They feel that abuse and neglect is the problem of "those" people—the ones who abuse and neglect their children. If you really believe child abuse and neglect is someone else's problem, that it doesn't concern you, and if you are not even curious about some possible solutions to the problem, then this book is not for you.

However, if you read on, you will note that child abuse and neglect is clearly *our* problem—yours and mine. Why?

1

Because everyone is responsible for America's most precious resource—our children. But there is another reason. In this book you will also notice a very fine line exists—some say it is only a matter of definition—between out-of-control behavior toward children and abuse of children. If you and I are honest, we will admit that our world is not always calm and serene. We experience those moments, moods, and situations that point out the fine balance between being in control of a situation and being out of control. When pushed to our limits and beyond, we may use actions, words, and behaviors we regret later. The clear realization dawns that at some point and under some circumstances we are all capable of child abuse and neglect. So if we have this capability, we also have the capability to stop it—to do something about this complex problem.

Where do we start? What is the first step? How can we avoid being overwhelmed by our task? The intelligent way to approach any problem such as this is to find out everything we can about the issue to have a baseline of facts from which to work.

You have taken that important first step toward gathering those facts by reading *Child Abuse: A Crying Shame.* This book has been written for parents, educators, day-care workers, youth workers, students, and friends of children everywhere who want to learn the basic facts about child abuse and neglect as well as some practical solutions to the problem.

Child abuse and neglect occurs every day—everywhere. The problem will not go away by itself. If we do not solve it, it will become our grim legacy. Read this book carefully and ask probing questions about your role in stopping abuse and neglect. In the future all of us will pay a dear price for allowing our children to be abused and neglected. And we can stop it. We must stop it.

1
What Is Child Abuse and Neglect?

~When Jerry, a six-year-old, bent over the drinking fountain, belt marks were clearly visible on his neck and arms. His father had beaten him ~~when he refused to spell "butterfly" correctly~~.

— Cindy, a one-year-old, was brought to the sitters with small, round cigarette burns on the palms of her hand. ~~Her mother was teaching her to leave the new plant alone~~.

Diane, a fourth grader, is always waiting on the school steps in the morning, and she is the last one to leave in the afternoon. Her mother works long hours, and Diane is afraid to stay in the apartment alone.

— Jimmy, a second-grader, has missed more school than he has attended the last few months. His hair is matted, his teeth

3

are decayed, and his clothes are spotted. Other children taunt him and say he smells. His parents are alcoholics and don't take care of him.

Kathy, a junior high girl, becomes more and more withdrawn in school. She is now four months pregnant. The father of the baby is Kathy's own father, who has been sleeping with her for over a year. Kathy's mother has known about the situation but is afraid of being beaten if she says anything about it.

Today in our child-loving, youth-oriented society, incidents of child abuse and neglect have reached epidemic proportions. Abuse is now considered to be the leading cause of death among children. Every four hours, child abuse claims another life.

Children are suffering verbal attacks, abandonment, rejection, sexual abuse, and physical injury by every possible object to every part of their bodies. They are being burned, strangled, shot, or starved by mothers and fathers. Others endure neglect, emotional battering, or solitary confinement. Under these conditions, some children die. Those who live may be psychologically damaged for life.

Examples of abuse and neglect include every cruel act imaginable—some of them beyond our imagination. Although distressing case studies will not be detailed here, it is enough to say that they *have* happened, they *are* happening, and they *will continue* to happen unless we all pull together to stop them.

This book is written for those parents, teachers, and friends of children everywhere who believe that tomorrow's world is in our children's hands. We believe that children are the most precious, valuable resource we have for the future. So, in order for tomorrow's world to be a better place, today's children must have the very best childhood experiences possible—including optimal physical growth and personal development, free from fear of abuse or neglect.

Child abuse and neglect cannot continue. In fact, nearly 1½ billion reasons why we must stop child abuse and neglect are under the age of ten.

In order to better understand our mission for the future, we must first study the history of child abuse and neglect. That understanding will help us design a stronger base for identification, action, and prevention.

History of Child Abuse

Child abuse is not a phenomenon of the twentieth century, nor is it unique to our society and culture. It has occurred throughout the recorded history of man. It exists today in many nations, cutting across language barriers, social and cultural mores, and political ideologies. Historical overviews show that often children had more brutality than love in their lives. Killing female infants once was such a common practice that many societies had a male population four or five times greater than the female population. In some cultures only one female member of a family was spared. The practice of killing infants continued well into the Middle Ages in Europe and Asia. Although it eventually disappeared as a common practice, physical abuse did not. In sixteenth-century Europe, doctors wrote of infants with broken bones from the "game" of tossing them about for amusement. The well-known eighteenth-century philosopher Jean Jacques Rousseau wrote that beatings were a common way to keep children quiet. However, he obviously had a concern about these circumstances, for he wrote, "Let us speak less of the duties of children and more of their rights" (R. Helfer and C. Kempe 1974).

Emotional abuse and neglect were often as severe as physical abuse. Soon after birth, many children were given over to wet nurses or servants for rearing without much contact with their parents. Other children were forced into skill training or apprenticeships at the age of five or six.

6

The common practice of some wealthy families was to use slave children for their personal sexual pleasure. One does not have to look back too far to find evidence of both male and female children employed in brothels.

In the United States, also not too many years ago, an established practice allowed seven- and eight-year-old children to work in coal mines. Only a few individuals who had a more humane perception of human development and social growth protested these circumstances.

Slowly civilization is learning that children are a precious resource for the future—that they must have the basic rights to grow and mature to their fullest potential. To do this, they must be free from the fear of abuse and neglect.

Some landmark dates in the history of child abuse and neglect include the following:

1875: The New York City Society for the Prevention of Cruelty to Children (SPCC) was initiated. Within five years, similar organizations were formed in New York State, New Hampshire, California, Massachusetts, and Pennsylvania.

1890: Children's Aids Societies were formed to help bands of homeless youths working as newsboys or as shoeshine boys in urban areas. These boys were sleeping in alleys, in parks, or on docks. The customary practice was to send them to foster homes, usually with farm families, where they were often exploited as cheap labor rather than being given secure or loving homes.

1909: The White House Conference on Children recognized an important fact: working with parents to prevent recurring abuse and neglect is a vital function of child protection services. The earlier philosophy was not to provide social services but simply to rescue the children and punish the abusing parents. This date marks a philosophical turning point in the care and treatment of the abused child and his family.

1912: The National Children's Bureau, now part of the Department of Health, Education and Welfare, was formed to provide leadership and national planning on child-related issues.

1917: President Woodrow Wilson signed the child labor legislation into law. Although the laws would later be declared unconstitutional, and a subsequent constitutional amendment to limit child labor failed to be ratified by the required number of states, child labor laws eventually were enacted that withstood court challenges. Many remain in force today.

1922: By this year 57 SPCC chapters and 307 humane societies in the nation protected children. These organizations carried much of the responsibility for child protective services until the 1940s, when public agencies gradually began to take over this task.

1968: By 1968 all fifty states had enacted some form of law regarding the reporting of child abuse cases to authorities— usually the police or the welfare department. By the 1960s the belief that most abusing parents would take advantage of services when available had largely replaced the discredited punitive philosophy of the early twentieth century.

1968: Mayor John Lindsay appointed what was to be the state's first task force on child abuse in New York City. Dr. Vincent Fontana, a pediatrician who published one of the earliest texts on child abuse in 1964, *The Maltreated Child*, was largely responsible for bringing the problem to Lindsay's attention. The task force recommended a computerized city-wide central register for reporting suspected cases of child abuse.

1974: The Child Abuse Prevention and Treatment act (PL93-247 [see Appendix]) was signed into law. This national legislation created the National Center on Child Abuse and Neglect. This legislation came after a decade of concerted efforts by leading authorities to expose the problem to the public. Among those who campaigned for federal action were Dr. C. Henry Kempe (a pediatrician and author of *The Battered Child*), Dr. Vincent J. Fontana (*The Maltreated Child*) and David Gil, a sociologist whose early research led to the first shocking estimates of the scope of abuse and neglect.

1975: Pennsylvania's Child Protective Services Act was passed by the General Assembly and signed by the governor. This act creates a free, around-the-clock, statewide hotline called Child Line, to receive reports of suspected child abuse. This protective services act was considered a prototype in the United States. After the Child Line began operating in Pennsylvania, many changes in reporting were discovered. In fact, the reports of child abuse increased 126 percent from 1975 to 1976 and another 102 percent from 1976 to 1977, the first full year of Child Line operation. Through Child Line, Pennsylvania reported they were beginning to look below the tip of the iceberg and locate many child-abuse cases that never would have been revealed if reporting procedures had not been improved (Kempe and Helfer 1972).

Definitions

It is difficult to separate child abuse from child neglect. In many circumstances a neglectful situation is at the same time a psychologically abusive situation. And, on the other hand, a child suffering from a pattern of physical abuse may not be eating properly, may have been expelled from his home, and is probably not attending school regularly. So in many situations an abusive circumstance creates a neglective situation, and vice versa.

Child Abuse

overhead

The law gives us a "bare-bones" definition of child abuse, and child neglect is included as a part of it. The Child Abuse Prevention and Treatment Act (PL93-247) describes child abuse as follows: "Physical or mental injury, sexual abuse, negligent treatment or maltreatment of a child under the age of 18 by a person who is responsible for the child's welfare under circumstances which indicate that the child's health or welfare is harmed or threatened."

Neglect

It is usually agreed that the term *neglect* includes withholding necessary food, clothing, shelter, and educational opportunities, or other forms of inadequate care and supervision that might lead to endangering the child's well-being. Neglect also means withholding love, socialization, and proper stimulation. Such withholding hinders a child's proper growth and development. The term *failure to thrive* describes this type of neglect. It is a diagnostic category of infants who suffer from severe malnutrition and developmental lags. These babies are often irritable and apathetic; they may vomit and have diarrhea (Child Welfare League 1974).

The parents of these infants may have poor support systems, may appear alienated from each other, may seem somewhat depressed, and may have few close relationships. Perhaps the mother is more concerned with child rearing "methods" than with human nurturing. Some people have tended to view child neglect as different from and less important than child abuse; but serious neglect *is* abuse and can have devastating effects on a child.

Child specialists contend that neglected children can suffer a greater intellectual handicap because of lack of stimulation than physically abused children. Often physically abused children have love, stimulation, and a positive relationship with parents even though at times the parents lash out and cannot control their emotions and impulsive actions.

Statistics

Statistics on child abuse and neglect may tell only a part of the story because, unfortunately, abuse and neglect are not as commonly reported as even less serious crimes. We'll discuss later some of the reasons why this is true, but it is enough to say that the statistics presented in this section may be significantly less than the true numbers. Even so, these conservative statistics are most impressive and truly distressing.

Abuse and Neglect

In 1978 one million children were abused in the United States. If the pattern continues, at least as many and probably a greater number will be abused each year. In 1978, as a direct result of child abuse, 5,000 children died. These figures will probably also increase. In the United States today child battering is the number one common cause of death in children—a shocking statistic when one considers the fatal auto and home accidents and the infectious diseases from which children die.

Conservative estimates indicate that two to fifteen children die each day from physical abuse, and a great many more are permanently handicapped—either emotionally, physically, or mentally. According to Vincent J. Fontana, early promoter of action against child abuse and neglect and author of numerous books on the subject (Martin 1978).

Frank Osanka (1979), also an authority on abuse statistics, revealed that seven children die each day of abuse, and the majority of them are between birth and three years of age. Brain damage may cripple a child for life. Twelve children each day suffer brain damage from some sort of abuse. It is additionally distressing to suspect that there may be as many as three times these figures in unreported cases. "If behavior patterns of the American family continue in this way, the body count will be higher than that of the Vietnam War," stated Dr. Osanka. He believes that parents who can't cope with the challenges as well as the frustrations and who don't get help and adequate resources from agencies and communities will give us other historical figures like Lee Harvey Oswald, Charles Manson, and James Wilkes Booth. There is evidence that all of these men were victims of some form of child abuse and neglect.

A leading child-abuse authority, Ray Helfer (Shanas 1975), predicts that "unless changes are made in prevention and treatment, there will be millions of reported cases of child abuse in the next 10 years [including] 50,000 deaths and 30,000 permanently injured children—most of whom will be brain damaged" (p. 482).

Let us consider some of the costs of child abuse to our society. Injuries to the head and central nervous system are usually among the most common forms of physical injury suffered by abused children. The cost of caring for one permanently brain-injured child in a public facility for one year is $15,162. If that child lives for another forty-seven years, the cost to the taxpayer is $712,614. The cost of caring for one permanently brain-injured child in a private facility for one year is $28,800. If that child lives for an additional forty-seven years, the cost is $1,353,600.

The most common form of treatment for child abuse ordered by a court is temporary foster care. The cost of foster care for one child for one year is $4,500, and the average length of foster care is four years.

Now let us consider the costs of another abuse-related factor. In recent years, researchers have noted a connection between child abuse and juvenile delinquency. The cost of sheltering one juvenile for one year is $8,900. A high correlation exists also between child abuse and the commission of felonies by adults. The cost of incarcerating one adult for one year is $6,500 (Frazer 1978).

From these statistics we can agree that in terms of dollars the cost is staggering. However, the cost in terms of the loss of future productive citizens is even greater. We may be able to measure the dollar cost, but our tools are not sophisticated enough to measure the pain and suffering caused by child abuse and neglect. We will probably never be able to make that measure.

Abuse and Poverty

The thread that connects poverty to abuse and abuse to poverty is thin. However, if you were to analyze an average caseload of abusive families, you would perceive low income, dependence on public aid, and marginal employment as common factors. In 1976 almost half of the reported cases of abuse and neglect were in homes with an income of less than $5,000 per year (The Nation's Health 1978).

The cycle of poverty and abuse may be important, but other factors must be considered before we assume too much. When abuse occurs in families who have little money, the most common place they turn to for treatment is a state or county clinic or hospital. The staff at the facility is trained to look for suspected cases of abuse. So the inquiries take place, and the report is made.

Now consider the average- or above average-income family. If abuse occurs in this family, they may go to their private doctor, or they may choose to shop for a different doctor each time abuse occurs. Since private doctors often have a lower rate of reporting suspected abuse cases than do doctors from clinics or public facilities, abuse cases in average- or above-average income families may go unreported.

The important point is that parents of all income levels need help in coping with the day-to-day problems of rearing children. But those parents who have the extra stress of only marginal resources need immediate, accessible support systems to rely on in times of crisis.

That thin thread between poverty and abuse may or may not tie the two together. Many authorities believe, as in other situations, the crimes of the poor are so much more visible than the crimes of the rich. Parents in the middle- or upper-income bracket may never be reported because of their ability to "doctor-shop," or, when all else fails, to hire a good lawyer to represent their case.

Types of Abuse and Neglect

If someone asked you, "What is child abuse?" you would probably reply, "It's physical damage done to a child." You'd be correct in your reply, and most people would respond just as you did. Physical beatings of children are visible, brutal, and all too common. However, in this section we will discuss not only the physical types of abuse and neglect but also the less visible but equally tragic kinds of abuse, such as sexual, emotional, social, and educational.

Physical Abuse and Neglect

When a parent or caretaker nonaccidentally inflicts injury to a child, it is considered physical abuse. Even a slap inflicted by an upset parent, especially if it is out of proportion to the offense, is abuse. Although a physical beating is the most common type of abuse, other abusive action may be any of the following: kicking, shooting, stabbing, scalding, burning, strangling, chaining, freezing, shaking, throwing, and dropping the body. Any form of physical action that causes cuts, bruises, or psychological distress is considered physical abuse.

Some child-abuse authorities insist that hitting the child with anything other than the hand is abusive action. They believe a very fine line exists between over-disciplining and abusive action. Their point is that if spanking is done only

with the hand, a human limit exists to the force behind it—
also a limit to the number of times it happens. In other
words, the hand will begin to sting and burn with repeated
action, and the spanking will cease. Many abusive parents
have said, "I forgot how many times I hit my child; it
couldn't have been more than three or four times." However,
an investigation of the situation reveals that the parent
blanked out fifteen or twenty times after the first three or
four. If a stick, a cord, a brush, or some other type of weapon
is used, the difference between three or four and fifteen or
twenty is child abuse.

Child-abuse authorities are also concerned with the part of
the child's body that is hit in a disciplining situation. For
example, if a child is slapped or hit around the face or head,
tiny hemmorrhages can occur all over the brain. Even one
such blow can cause mild to severe forms of mental
retardation. Also, shaking, throwing, or dropping the body
can cause severe brain damage because young children's
heads are softer, and they do not instinctively protect
themselves as older children do.

Nearly everyone has had the experience of reaching out
affectionately to ruffle a child's hair, when suddenly out of
instinct the child ducks and protects himself with his hands.
This child may or may not have been slapped or hit about
the head at some point in his life. Although it may be a
sobering incident at the time, we can't assume too much.
Many families roughhouse in such a playful way as to make
instinctive physical protection a natural act.

Sexual Abuse and Neglect

Sexual exploitation of children, thought uncommon, is
probably the most underdiagnosed type of child abuse.
Incest, long regarded as a taboo subject, has been assumed to
be a rare and isolated occurrence. However, it is increasingly
gaining recognition as a social problem of significant
proportions in many sectors of our society. Despite the

prevalence of the problem, few treatment programs aim specifically at helping incestuous families. Those communities having such a treatment program nearly always stimulate a significant increase in the reporting rate, leading authorities to agree it may be the highest unreported crime in our country.

Let us define the terms and actions that go together to constitute the broader term *sexual abuse.* Incest is defined as sexual intercourse between a child and a related adult. Sexual molestation is defined as sexual contact short of intercourse, such as exposure, touching, or masturbation. Sexual neglect is defined as failure to prevent someone from engaging in sexual activities with a child.

Incest and sexual molestation have been termed a basic violation of the family code. Sigmund Freud wrote that every child develops a natural barrier against incest as a part of society's cultural demands. The child learns that blood relations—the person he or she has loved from birth—are off limits as sexual objects. Freud also believed that children would have an easier time finding other love objects if the parents' affections didn't awaken children's sexual instincts prematurely (Kay, 1978).

In violating this basic family code, sexual abuse and molestation is also an assault on a child's constitutional rights, his body space, his psychological space, and his healthy emotional and sexual development.

Conservative sources estimate over a quarter of a million sexual abuses and molestations across the country each year. In most cases the victimized child is a girl, and over half of these children are under age twelve at the time of the offense. The statistics also say that one in four females, or 25 to 35 percent of all females, will be sexually abused by the time they are eighteen.

Although most research suggests young females are victimized more than young males, some new data suggests that boys are assaulted as often as girls. Dr. Carolyn Swift

(January 1979) told a subcommittee of the U.S. House of
Representatives that data on sexually abused boys has been
ignored by the "primarily male" medical community. She
cited research over the past forty years to document
substantial numbers of sexually victimized boys. Swift's
concern is that through this oversight victimized boys have
been deprived of treatment. Her point is that too few
treatment programs exist for victims of sexual abuse, and
most of them are directed toward young females.

According to Swift, "There appear to be degrees of
deviance, with concomitant degrees of taboo, within the area
of sexual exploitations of children as well as adults.
Homosexual attacks on children carry a double stigma since
they violate the heterosexual norm as well as the prohibition
of the use of a child as a sexual partner."

Swift cited one survey that reported "only 16.5 percent of
the sexually victimized boys told their parents, compared
with 43 [percent] of the victimized girls. . . . The message to
boys is that homosexual attacks are unspeakable events, more
humiliating than the female 'fate worse than death.' "

A majority of research studies, however, would still put
the highest percentage of sexual assaults in the male-adult
and the female-child category. A much smaller percentage
would be given to the male-male and female-female
relationships. Brother-sister relationships are less likely to be
reported because they tend to be handled by parents rather
than outside authorities.

Most studies overwhelmingly report that sexual abuse
begins in the home, and for many victims its horror becomes
a way of life. Everyone is shocked and appalled at the idea,
and probably asks "Why? How could anyone stoop so low as
to sexually abuse a child? What could possibly motivate such
deviant behavior?"

Out of certain treatment programs across the country—and
they are too few—has come one picture of the incestuous
family situation: The family is dislodged from its roots. It is

thrown on its own resources with no ties to the society around it. The father doesn't feel connected to any community. Perhaps the job is new and not going well, and perhaps the marriage is not going well, either. He perceives the daughter as "available," the only warm creature around. She won't reject him. She is not threatening. Out of a need to feel close to someone comes the father's sexual motivation.

Parents in therapy have given many possible reasons for incestuous relations. One man told his wife their daughter "reminds me of you ten years ago." Another blamed it on liquor. One said his wife wouldn't have him, so he took their oldest daughter. These comments probably represent many similar explanations of the "why" of an incestuous relationship.

Many men blame their actions on the children, saying they provoked them to it. Psychiatrists and social workers say after years of favors, bribes, secrets, and seduction, an adolescent could learn to be provocative. However, those who work with victimized youth seldom can remember any young person's accusation that turned out to be unfounded. The experience is horrifying to them personally as it is to everyone involved in the investigation.

Perhaps the "why" of incestuous relationships can best be explained by the view some people hold toward others. If a perpetrator feels that his victim is subservient or is his property to do with as he wishes, sexual assault can occur and can continue to occur.

What are some of the consequences to sexually abused children? Dr. F. Osanka (1979) suggests that this type of abuse may manifest itself in many ways. Abused adolescents may marry before they are ready as a means of escaping a disastrous home situation. Research shows that the married lives of sexually abused children are frequently marked by sexual dysfunction. If they reported the abuse and legal action became the result, they might feel tremendous guilt or responsibility for the destruction of the accused member of the family and the family unit. Often young victimized females turn to promiscuity in their search for affection. In effect, they may be saying to their parents, "I'll get back at you because you deserted me." It is possible that two trusted figures have failed them: the abusing father and the neglectful mother who failed to help when she was needed most. In the case of runaway juveniles, the possibility of sexual abuse and neglect must always be considered. One professional youth worker complained, "It's an incredible system that locks up its children for running away from an intolerable family situation."

The consequences of sexual abuse to very young children are equally distressing. Some treatment programs first try to help a child clarify realities. For example, no four-year-old child can be responsible for seducing an adult. The responsibility clearly lies with the adult. Yet often children as young as three and four years of age think it is their fault. They believe they have done something wrong to make it happen. So the first step must be an attempt to help a child understand it was not her behavior that caused the abuse. This is not an easy task. Explaining and working through such a complex situation in adult therapy is difficult enough, but achieving success with a three- or four-year-old child seems impossible. One must have considerable respect for the staff in such treatment programs and hope they have a superhuman amount of insight, patience, and compassion.

Some authorities who work with sexual-abuse statistics say that incest has a very low visibility. It is kept hidden in the family, and unless a crisis occurs, it does not surface. Unfortunately, usually the crisis emerges on the child's shoulders in the form of a pregnancy, a runaway from home, or a severe drop in school grades. In such a crisis, questions should be asked and inquiries made to get to the motivation for the action that produced the crisis. Sometimes the real reasons are offered, but many times victims are too fearful or embarrassed to tell the truth.

Authorities say another reason sexual-abuse statistics are hard to obtain is that incest cases are often prosecuted as child molestation, statutory rape, or forcible rape, and the basic issue of child abuse is skirted.

Scant literature is available about sexual abuse, particularly concerning successful treatment. Programs especially created to deal with abusing families must be innovative in drawing upon social resources and adapting them to meet the needs of the community. Often, programs designed to treat families involved in sexual abuse are not funded because the community does not see sexual abuse as a problem in their area. If statistics can be gathered, the need becomes apparent. However, as we mentioned, accurate statistics are elusive.

Probably the most important truth about the whole area of sexual abuse is that each person in the community can provide support to sexually abused children. It's important that helping adults be available in the most unlikely situations or at the most unexpected times. Professionals and lay persons need to provide a warm but clinical presence and to maintain an objective distance and a flexibility when they listen to the story of sexual abuse. It is a most difficult assignment. However, in dealing with either the parent or the child, one should not indicate shock, surprise, or offense; for such reaction may immediately inhibit any further meaningful communication. Instead, the adult should attempt to encourage the victim to relate all the details of the situation. These comments should later be recorded precisely because often the person in crisis becomes frightened and attempts to retract them. These data should then be turned over to authorities, such as Child Protective Services, so that they can intervene on the victim's behalf.

As family stress becomes more and more a part of our everyday existence, problems relating to sexual molestation and abuse will probably increase. However, not even the experts can say if incest is increasing, but they do agree that a greater number of instances are being reported. Even the most hardened public anguishes over a sexually abused child. But as one school counselor said when the offender turned out to be a father, "These are the cases that make our brains go crazy." Community awareness and understanding is certainly a first step toward solving this problem. In later chapters we will discuss reporting procedures and successful treatment programs.

Emotional Abuse and Neglect

Emotional abuse comes in many forms and disguises, such as the following: teasing, yelling, desertion, disinterest, name-calling, down-grading, continual criticism, scary threats, and any other behavior that destroys or damages a child's self-esteem or his self-image.

The type of emotional abuse that is especially detrimental is verbal abuse that bombards the child until he not only has lost his self-esteem but develops a negative self-image because of constant negative reinforcement. The child who constantly hears that he's a "no-good, dumb kid" eventually responds like a "no-good, dumb kid" and soon begins to believe it.

Emotional abuse can also express itself in a nonverbal way, such as the parent or caretaker giving a child "the silent treatment." Often disinterest and silence go hand-in-hand. Children may then act in negative ways to get attention. If the child uses consistent negative, attention-getting behavior, he may also receive physical abuse. In other words, the child who gets slapped or beaten feels that abuse is better than the silent treatment.

In emotional abuse, the difference between normal and abnormal is hard to define. Many normal parents yell and even scream at their children. However, some children are scapegoated, berated, and rejected on a daily basis. This is abnormal treatment. You may ask, "But how do you go about proving something like that?" It is extremely difficult.

Teachers and counselors can work on the premise that the child who is severely emotionally abused at home will probably be emotionally disturbed in the classroom and will have difficulty with schoolwork. This child will also have an emotional blocking of his thought processes. When asked a difficult question or asked to perform in a particular way, he may think, "I'm stupid, dumb, no-good. I can't do anything right." So instead of trying to answer the question or do the task, the child has a defeatist attitude at the outset, and his emotions block his ability to think.

A child who is overly aggressive at school and exhibits bullylike behavior is often being bullied at home by parents or others. If you question this type of behavior in a private setting, you may hear stories of harsh discipline and unrelenting rules. If parents are enforcing unrealistic rules the child can't cope with and are meting out harsh discipline if the child fails to comply, the child is constantly in trouble. Without correction of this problem, the child may end up battered and may have severe nervous disorders, or at least serious emotional difficulties. Emotional abuse takes its toll in many different ways.

Social Abuse and Neglect

Although social abuse may not have as severe consequences as the other types of abuse we've discussed, it is no less destructive to a child's potential for development. Social abuse can begin very early. Overly conscientious parents may protect their child to the point that the child doesn't have normal day-to-day learning experiences, social interaction, and emotional development. Some parents are so worried about their child's becoming contaminated in some way that they avoid all outside contacts. They tend to isolate themselves and their child. This situation doesn't always manifest itself with first-time parents either, as one might think. Even at school age, a child may be kept so close to home that he never learns to get along with others. Parents may say, "We are the only friends you need."

A child's natural curiosity is a strong motivating force toward learning. If he is constantly held back, protected, and denied new experiences, he will eventually give up trying new things. In order to participate fully in life and grow to his potential, a young child must have an "I can do it; I can try new things and be successful" feeling. The only way he learns he can be successful is by having his curiosity satisfied through adventuresome experiences.

Some parents don't allow their child to play with other children in the neighborhood; they thus deny him the friends and playmates necessary to him for proper social development. Mom may say, "I don't want you to have anything to do with those kids. They aren't like us. They're different and bad!" A parent's prejudiced attitudes, values, and feelings, purposely taught to a child, are also a form of social abuse. Children need to interact, to play, and to get along with all kinds of people. They need experiences that broaden, not narrow, their outlook on life.

Everyone has seen the child in the shopping center, in the supermarket, or at school with food on his face, with dirty hair, with a disheveled appearance and inadequate clothing for the weather. It is not an uncommon sight. So, one might say, these problems are commonplace and must be tolerated. However, when a child's hygiene is so neglected that he smells of urine or stool, when he is teased and ostracized by his peer group, the problem has reached the point of social abuse, and something must be done about it. The child's parents or caretakers need to be interviewed and encouraged to help improve their child's hygiene. The normal parent would be concerned if his child were being made the laughingstock of the classroom. Parents who profess no concern and back up their statement with a lack of action need help and consultation.

Another type of social abuse or neglect is nutritional deprivation—a term to describe a child who is malnourished because of deliberate underfeeding by his parents. Some underweight children are thin on a genetic basis, like their parents. However, the child about whom we should be concerned is the one who is not only underweight but who also reports that he has no breakfast at home, brings meager lunches to school, or consumes huge quantities of the school lunch.

An appropriate first step is to ask the parents to provide their child a breakfast and a more adequate lunch. If parents don't have the breakfast habit, if the child is a finicky breakfast eater, and if time is of short supply, parents may dismiss food as unnecessary. However, these parents usually need only one such reminder from the school nurse or teacher to change their morning food pattern. If parents repeatedly fail to carry out the recommendations, something needs to be done.

Another type of social abuse occurs when a parent deliberately shares dangerous drugs or alcohol with a child. If a child mentions frequent drug usage, and signs indicate he is becoming an addict, a teacher or a neighbor must do something about the situation. Failure to do so could result in the child's experiencing a serious overdose or a blackout, and permanent physical damage could result.

Many children need eyeglasses, dental work, or immunizations. Sometimes parents put these unpleasant things off because of lack of time or money or because of the disagreeable scene the child might make. Usually a doctor or a school nurse's advice is enough to prod the parents into action. Sometimes ringworm or impetigo gets out of control. Sometimes a child suddenly begins to favor an arm or a leg; then a reminder from the nurse or a teacher is necessary. Social abuse becomes critical when you have talked with the parent and no action is taken; you've tried setting up appointments, and the parent doesn't show up; you've arranged for financial assistance, and the parent doesn't act.

The helpful approach rarely fails; but if it does, the problem can be turned over to the child protective agency.

Educational Abuse and Neglect

Laws to guarantee school attendance have long been in effect. The basic thinking is that with a proper education many a child can escape even a severely adverse home environment. So one important job that school personnel have is to make sure children do not needlessly miss regular schooling—especially in the early years when the basic fundamentals are being taught. Occasionally investigation into school truancy has revealed that a child is being confined to the home for work exploitation, sexual abuse, or even bizarre torture. With two-income families becoming more the rule than the exception, parents often ask their junior high or high-school-age child to care for the younger children. Certainly such an arrangement on an occasional basis is understandable, but when the older child begins to miss several days of school at a time or drops out completely, educational abuse may be occurring, and some action should be taken.

Educational programs that do not fit a child's needs may also be a type of educational abuse. Not every child can or should be taught the same things in the same way. Educators have often spoken out about individualizing instruction and personalizing teaching so that children can learn in the style most appropriate for them. However, one does not have to spend much time in an elementary or junior high school to observe that most teachers are lecturing the entire class on the same subject, using the same method for all. Teachers are "under the gun" to follow the manual, complete the text, and drill for regularly administered tests. As a result, many children view themselves as failures and find themselves considered so by classmates because they can't complete the set tasks at the same speed as others. So, like many, they give up, turn off, reject, search for ways of behaving in which they can succeed, however inappropriate. Teachers do not get all the blame in this problem, and the indictment is not directed at all teachers. However, many teachers could devote more creative time and energy to either the very fast or the very slow students in their classrooms.

Psychologists continue to warn us against emotional abuse in the form of placing constant pressure and stress on children. Some examples of this type of school pressure are comparison with others (grades or other marks), class assignments that are too complex for some (repetitious trivia for others); indiscriminate homework requiring the same task of every child in the classroom; teacher-conducted tests of physical skills that favor a few at the expense of less coordinated students; and admonitions to young children to "act like an adult" or "act grown up."

One way adults can lessen school pressures is to insist on smaller class size so that teachers can accomplish a more individualized approach. Another way is for educators to encourage teachers in teacher-education institutions to become more knowledgeable about the nature of learning and the developmental aspects of human beings. Then all of us, teachers included, must clearly articulate our beliefs to administrators, to parents, and to school boards. Teachers need all the support they can get to prohibit educational abuse in their classrooms.

Let us look at educational abuse from a totally different point of view. Parents who bring children into this world without a serious thought about how they are going to rear them are practicing a form of educational abuse. These parents do not understand the important milestones of their child's growth and development; so they don't really know what to expect. Often, totally unrealistic expectations occur as a result. The schools, the church, and the home should combine to train future parents. After the baby arrives is still not too late for parenting education, but ideally it should occur all through the parent's own childhood.

"I told you, the stork brought you!" and "What you don't know won't hurt you!" are two comments that may also contribute to educational abuse. Parents who refuse to discuss sex with their child, who perpetuate myths and untruths about human sexuality, and who generally put their heads in the sand, are guilty of educational abuse. When they refuse to educate their child about his or her body and how it functions, they abuse and neglect that child. A majority of parents find it difficult to give the "birds and bees" lecture when their children are at age ten or eleven because they themselves haven't had the "body function and sexuality" talks. Since proper sex education occurs slowly over a long period of observation, curiosity, and questioning, it must begin the day a child is born.

Sex education is difficult for many parents because of their basic lack of understanding about their own sexuality. They are uncomfortable about discussing the topic; so they brush it aside or ignore a child's early inquiries. It doesn't take a child long, then, to realize sex is a taboo subject; so he goes elsewhere for this vital information. Many times the information the child gets from his peers or on the street is not correct in nature or has a vulgar twist to it.

Sex education must start early and should be taught in the home. Failure to do this is a form of child abuse and neglect.

Child Snatching—the New Child Abuse

The scene is usually set following a rough divorce trial and a bitter custody fight: things are starting to settle into visitations on a regular basis, and suddenly one parent has vanished with the children. Thousands of dollars may be spent on the services of a private detective, to no avail. Frustrations, emotions, and anxiety build as the abandoned parent keeps asking, "Will they remember me? Are they safe? Healthy?" If they were very young when they were taken, the parent is quite sure they won't remember, and that probably hurts the most.

To steal one's own child is not an act of love. The basic motivation is selfishness. Often the divorce is so vengeful and bitter all the parent can think of is to try to sever all contact with the spouse. Weekly visitation rights are a constant visual reminder of the past, and in complete desperation a parent grabs the child and runs. Because of variance in state laws, prosecution is very difficult, although proposed legislation may equalize these laws.

Suffice it to say, for whatever reason or however strong the motivation, child snatching is a form of child abuse. A child deserves access to both parents during the important childhood and adolescent years.

Myths about Child Abuse

Some myths tend to hamper us in identifying and eventually putting a stop to abusive action. Some of these myths are long-standing and will not be broken down quickly, but if we examine them and discuss them, perhaps it will be a first step toward dispelling them.

The child-oriented society myth may be the single greatest impediment to reducing child abuse. It says that America is a youth-focused society that is meeting the needs of even our smallest members; whereas in fact, many of the basic rights of children are being violated every day. If we believe the conservative estimates of two to fifteen child-abuse deaths each day, we realize that the basic right to life laid out by our constitutional fathers is being denied. Many other examples point to the fact that we are not catering to our youth's needs. For example, even though we have some of the most modern technology in the world, the United States doesn't even rank among the ten nations having the lowest incidence of infant mortality and of mothers dying in childbirth.

Millions of American children receive only marginal health care and often fail to get the proper vaccines, even though they have long been accessible and inexpensive. Outbreaks of measles are common, and leading health authorities warn of possible epidemics of long-disappearing diseases, such as polio and smallpox.

Persistent malnutrition hampers many children from learning to their maximum potential. A hungry stomach can block out all educational input and can handicap a child mentally, physically, and socially.

Millions of children still spend their childhood in custodial institutions and group homes. Many of these homes provide the basics for proper growth and development. However, others are little more than "holding areas" that temporarily keep a child until something more permanent can be arranged. With our court system overloaded and our social services moving slowly, "temporary" often becomes "permanent."

Another popular myth is the *biologic ability to parent myth*. This myth, universally accepted, states that if you have the biologic ability to *have* a child, then you automatically know *how* to be a parent. It's a nonthinking myth that many young people believe to be truth. Some high schools offer parenthood classes with practical work in nursery schools or day care centers. However, only a few boys and not all girls can take this opportunity. Parenting is not an automatic skill or a talent that suddenly emerges at the birth of a child.

The *Gerber Baby myth* is a closely related untruth often held by young parents or parents-to-be. It says that all babies are soft and clean and never scream. It also holds that when babies are born, they look like the ones in the television ads and in the magazine displays. Anyone around a newborn nursery for very long knows that when babies are born they are not always beautiful and certainly not quiet. More often, the picture-perfect, model "newborns" in the ads are really two or three months old, filled out and on their best behavior.

The *Madonna myth* goes along with the Gerber Baby myth in that it states that mothers are always beautiful, loving, calm, cool, and smiling. Obviously, these myths are not true to life. Families have their ups and downs. Crisis situations are not uncommon with young parents and young children.

A dangerous myth that can foster child abuse more than any other is the *children as property myth*. This myth goes something like this: "Children are the property of their parents"; "A child should be seen and not heard"; "A man's home is his castle." This type of thinking promotes an abnormal parent-child relationship in that it disregards the child as a person with basic rights. The rationale that a parent can do anything he wants in his own home perpetuates the avoidance of responsibility on the part of neighbors, friends, and the community. This behavior is not just a personal problem but a community responsibility that requires active community involvement and participation.

Finally, the *It's the other person myth* covers probably everyone who reads this book. One tends to think of child abusers as "those people" rather than considering that under given circumstances and conditions, "it could be me."

Child abuse and neglect cuts across all social, economic, educational, and cultural lines. Exactly half of all child abuse is committed by men, the other half by women. Abusers include people on welfare as well as well-paid professionals, high school drop-outs, those with advanced degrees, and all ethnic groups.

Perhaps the universality of child abuse is summed up by the recent book released by the daughter of a famous actress (Crawford 1979). The specific points relative to this book were that child abuse is not limited to any one income group; one of the most unfortunate forms of child abuse is psychological and emotional abuse; and children who are abused may carry invisible scars well into adulthood and throughout their lives. The damage may not be visible, but it is there.

⚘ Why Is Child Abuse Such a Difficult Problem to Solve?

Some barriers to solving child-abuse and neglect problems have already been discussed, but others need to be stated here. Many of these problems will be expanded upon in later chapters.

- The cycle of abusive action is hard to break. For example, parents who have been themselves abused as children tend to abuse their own children in much the same way. The parenting model we use with our children is usually similar to the model we have seen as we were growing up in our own family. If a child in that family was threatened several times, then severely beaten as a general occurrence, probably that parent would respond to his own child in a similar way.

- Those parents or caretakers who might be potential abusers do not seek help because they are embarrassed, ashamed, and afraid to admit their acts. Most child abusers are normal people like you and me who act occasionally totally out of control. Potential abusers need help, but they have to identify themselves in order to get that help.

- Situations that result in child abuse are often uncontrollable. The caretaker usually copes with the child until things go wrong. For example, if a sudden crisis (like a job loss) occurs, if a new baby comes along, or if a family illness causes concern—and a child acts in a way the parent can't cope with, a potentially abusive situation arises. Also, conditions may slowly change over a period of time. A parent might gradually drink more alcohol, have financial problems, lose the ability to love or be loved, or lack the proper information about what to expect from children at each age level. Any combination of these might push the parent to abuse or neglect.

■ Information about child development and parenting is hard to get to the people who need it most. Someone said, "It's incredible that we have no special training, classes, or school to prepare adults for the most difficult job they'll ever have in their lives—that of being a parent." Although books, magazine articles, newsletters, courses, television programs, and many other ways exist for people to seek out parenting education and child-development information, a caretaker must have an interest in seeking them out.

■ Programs to help the whole family prevent abuse rather than treat the effects of it are usually not available to everyone. Often urban areas have these services, but few are available in rural areas.

■ One must always keep in mind that abusive action varies from family to family. What one might see as clear abuse or neglect another might label disciplinary punishment. Child abuse is not always a certainty.

■ Another difficulty in solving the problem is that not all cases are reported. In fact, authorities believe only a fraction of the total number of cases is reported.

■ Part of the reporting problem is that not all citizens know they can, should, and must report suspected or known cases of child abuse.

■ Finally, in this modern, enlightened age of ours, we want to do our own thing and not get involved with the distressing tragedies of others. With our knowledge and maybe even experience with the "I'll sue you!" process, we wash our hands of another human's hurts. Whether we can afford to do this or not is not the question. The question is, who stands to lose the most? The answer is always the same—the children.

2
Who Are
the Abusers

Our job of preventing child abuse and neglect would be much easier if we could put together a perfect profile of characteristics, stresses, and crises that fit every case. If we could determine what makes it happen each time, we could design some sure ways to prevent it from happening. Of course, this is impossible. Although each new research study adds a piece to the child-abuse puzzle, more often that puzzle piece points out another difference rather than a similarity. Because each human is an individual with a unique personality and a level of stress he must manage, each copes in different ways.

Looking at this problem objectively, we must admit that more of a continuum exists than a sharp distinction between those who abuse their children and those who do not. Imagine the continuum looking like this: on one end is the person who would never abuse a child under any circumstances; at the other end is the person who actually kills his child.

In the center of the continuum are most of us who occasionally exhibit insulting behavior toward a child, use excessive shouting to control, and even spank a bottom or two—behavior not viewed as child abuse.

Although we might all prefer to put as much distance as possible between ourselves and the "deviants" who abuse children, this continuum pretty clearly suggests that a good many of us would be capable of some sort of abuse if our environmental conditions, our pressure level, and our coping skills were sufficiently stressed.

Because of our individuality, no single model, factor, or set of factors can fully account for the occurrence of child abuse. Individuals and families who live under conditions of social stress identical to those of abusive families do not become abusers. Even children with characteristics identical to those of maltreated children do not become abused.

Why is this so? The paradox points to some type of a lively, constantly changing interplay among the adult, the child, and the environment. Therefore, as we discuss the characteristics of abusers and of the abused child, we must remind ourselves that each case is unique, each family reacts differently, and each societal unit provides an unusual situation. The problems of the abuser, the victim, and the world in which they live must have our concentration and focus in order for us to try to understand who the abusers are and why they do it.

Just as there is no one cause or characteristic of child abuse, neither can there be one type of treatment program that will work for all. No single approach can serve all the child abusers in our country—with its complex, varied population and its multiplicity of human personalities.

This is a warning to readers that the material to follow, specifically the section on characteristics of abusers and abused children, is presented as a guideline, not a recipe, for understanding the motivations and personality factors involved in child abuse and neglect.

Identifying Families at Risk

Although sufficient warnings have been given that we must evaluate each person and each environment differently, this is not sufficient reason to throw our hands in the air and say that little if anything can be done about the child-abuse problem. If we did that, we would all have tunnel vision concerning this issue. If we do not try to understand, if we do not seek solutions, if we stand by while child abuse and neglect continue to increase, we are all guilty of at least child neglect.

So we will attempt to identify some risk-related factors common to some, but not to all, potential abusers. Our basic purpose is to educate all of us, including those families who are potential child abusers, so that child abuse can be prevented. In other words, the problem must be identified, then eliminated before it occurs.

To help illustrate this point, we might take an example from the medical profession. Although heart disease can strike anyone, it is possible to identify several factors that increase the likelihood of a person's having it. Individuals who smoke, who are overweight, who do not exercise regularly, and who have a family history of heart disease are much more susceptible to heart disease than persons who do not fall into these categories. The basic idea of preventive medicine is to educate the high-risk population to danger signs and so lower the likelihood of heart disease.

The community has the responsibility to identify the potential child abuser and to work toward strengthening the family so that the problem can be eliminated.

Identifying Signs of Child Abuse and Neglect

As a medical doctor might look for clues in order to make an accurate diagnosis of disease, so neighbors, friends, educators, and youth workers can look for clues in considering a potential child abuser. The important fact to remember is that one sign by itself might not necessarily indicate an abuser. If a number of signs are present, however, concerned individuals have good reason to look further.

First, let's take a look at some of the situations that might occur in your own neighborhood, at school, at church, or in your community. Remember, child abuse occurs when many factors combine; so you will probably find many signs to identify child abuse and neglect. Let's look at the behavior of some parents.

In most neighborhoods the comings and goings of family members are pretty routine. Certain members go out in the morning and return in the evening. With some parents this is not the case. Ask yourself: Do certain parents stay out overnight? Are they gone for extended periods of time? Do their children ask neighbors for help with food or care? Do they say they do not know where their parents are? If so, these are signs of child abuse and neglect.

Is the family using alcohol or other drugs to excess? Are children being neglected or abused because of this abuse?

Perhaps you are a teacher who writes notes, telephones, or calls on parents concerning their child's welfare. Do the parents refuse to respond? Do they miss appointments and refuse to meet with you? If so, look more closely at their child for signs of abuse or neglect.

When you talk to parents about their child, are they evasive and indirect in their answers? Are they reluctant to share information about their child with you? If so, look for signs of abuse and neglect.

You may be concerned about a child's well-being, and you express those concerns to the parent. Does the parent show little concern for her child's problem? Does she shrug off your inquiry with, "He's always been that way. He'll grow out of it"? If you are really concerned, look for other signs of abuse and neglect.

Let's say you are a youth worker who notices a child has an injury. Do the parents take an unusually long time before seeking health care for the child who is hurting? Are they vague and embarrassed about explaining an injury? When you question them about the problem, do they complain about other problems unrelated to the injury? Do you get several different stories about how the injury occurred? Does the parent suggest that the cause of the injury was someone else's fault? If the answer is yes to all or a number of these questions, you may suspect child abuse and neglect.

Finally, let's say you approach a parent and ask a general question about the child's health, his bruises, his depression, or his aggressive behavior. Do the parents laugh it off with remarks that show they do not admit the seriousness of the problem? If so, look more closely for signs of child abuse and neglect.

Remember, child abuse occurs when several factors combine; so more than one sign might be visible.

Ask these questions:

Is little Karen thin, frail, emaciated-looking? Is she constantly complaining of being tired? Does her body show signs of malnutrition or dehydration?

Is Kenny dirty? Does he smell? Does he have bad teeth? Is his hair falling out? Does he have lice?

How is Karen dressed? Is her clothing soiled? Is it either too large or too small? Does she wear underwear? Is it changed regularly? Is she dressed inadequately for bad weather? Does she wear a thin jacket when it is very cold? Does she wear a long-sleeved shirt or sweater during the warm months?

Does Kenny complain about severe beatings? Does he describe razor straps, belts, sticks or other "weapons"?

Does Karen have an unusual number of "explained"

injuries, such as scratches, cuts, bruises, or burns on her legs
and arms over a period of time? Does she go to the bathroom
with difficulty? Does she complain that it hurts to urinate or
defecate? Does she complain that when mother is gone, the
boyfriend, the baby sitter, her uncle or brother "do things"?

Does Kenny talk about being given alcohol or other
drugs? Is he frequently away from school? Is he constantly
late? Or is he the first to arrive at school, at church, or at the
scout meetings? Is he the last to leave? Is he
uncommunicative? Does he seem to be withdrawn? Does he
seem not to care what happens to him? Is he shy? Is he
passive and compliant about everything going on around
him?

Does Karen act in a nervous manner? Is she destructive to
her own and others' belongings? Is she constantly talking,
laughing, and bothering others? Is she hyperactive? Finally, is
she instead fearful of new experiences? Is she fearful of
strangers? Is she afraid of other children or adults?

Many of these questions apply to children who are
growing up in happy families with plenty of love and
understanding—totally free from abuse and neglect. In other
words, at one time or another, all children behave, act, or
look like children described by these questions.

However, when you are looking for signs of child abuse
and neglect, these questions are a starting point. They can
send up warning flags that you should take a closer look.

Barrier: Conspiracy or Denial

One significant barrier to community involvement in
identifying families at risk is termed *the conspiracy of denial.*
We've all been involved in this conspiracy; it is alive and
well in American society. We don't want to hear about child
abuse, we dislike reading about it, we want to deny it's true.
Abusive parents deny maltreating their children. Even the
victims themselves deny having been abused. Why? One
answer is that children are often convinced they "deserved"

the abuse. They don't want to get their parents in trouble. They may fear their parents because they have been threatened with even worse abuse. They may be afraid they will be sent somewhere else to live.

Even doctors fall into the denial category. Physicians, especially those in private practice, are often reluctant to report cases of child abuse to the appropriate authorities. And if the patients are long-time acquaintances and have no history of abusive action, the physician may excuse it as a one-time event—nothing to get excited about.

Some family court judges routinely and automatically return abused children to their families regardless of the seriousness of the situation or without mandating any type of family therapy or treatment program. Returning a child to his family may be the best solution to the problem, but if it is done in a routine way without considering all the alternatives, the routineness becomes a form of denial.

Although schools are probably in the most strategic position to uncover cases of child abuse and neglect, many teachers avoid reporting such cases. They are reluctant to get involved because they feel they don't have the support or help of their administrators. Administrators say they don't have the backing of their school board or a written policy backing them up. And so it goes.

Everyone has reasons for denial, but none of the reasons help the identification, intervention, and prevention process.

Barrier: Privacy and Isolation

Another closely related barrier toward identifying families at risk is the isolation factor. To most of us, the value of privacy is unquestioned. If our privacy is invaded, whether the invasion is real or imagined, we cry foul. This value is reflected in our laws, in speeches of political candidates, in party platforms, in private agencies, and in public opinion polls. Although we hold this truth to be self-evident, some costs incur to both the individual and the community. One of the costs is paid by our children in the form of abuse and neglect (Garbarino 1977). For example, research on child abuse has shown a link between isolation and abusive behavior (Park and Collmer 1975). Several studies reported that a high proportion of abusing families lacked continuing relationships with others outside the family. Other studies have found that a majority of abusing families have unlisted telephone numbers. Some of those families have indicated the importance of solving problems or resolving crises on their own without the help of outsiders.

Sociologists help explain another piece of this isolation-and-abuse puzzle. They tell us that during past decades many young families have moved from the farm to small towns and from small towns to urban areas. The mobility of young families appears to be greater than it has ever been. In addition, young families have migrated to other states, particularly to the southern sunbelt areas, in search of jobs and a better lifestyle. Whether because of these migration patterns or other factors, another reason for isolation is that young families are not visited by or touched by kinfolk as once was the case. Families don't "go visiting" on a Sunday afternoon as they once did. Contrary to how Mom and Dad grew up, cousins may now grow to adulthood without ever knowing each other.

In the past, one's time and resources were always on call for kin in need. Relationships, family decisions, and day-to-day activities were under the watchful eye of Grandpa and Grandma, aunts and uncles, and sisters and brothers because everyone had a stake in the nuclear family. Childrearing practices were particularly noticed because if Johnny was too shy, or Susie was too spoiled, it was important to the welfare of the whole extended family. Some young families have used this closely-monitored atmosphere as a reason to move away. They have purposely erected barriers to interaction and involvement. They have taken steps to isolate themselves from their closest support group—their kin.

Another possible factor to consider on isolation is the growing trend for Americans to place a high value on independence, individualism, and the philosophy called "Do your own thing." Privacy is valued as an important ingredient for the achievement of this philosophy. For example, ownership of individual homes is still an American dream, in spite of high inflationary barriers. When ownership has been achieved, a six-foot fence is erected, and the newly isolated family lives within the walls, hugging their privacy. With this pattern of self-isolation, families become cut off from their neighbors, another potential support group besides kinfolk. In many neighborhoods in America, all one family knows about the other is the color of their car and their dog. Names, occupations, interests, abilities, and needs are privileged information.

Other examples suggest that middle-class families have traded kinship and neighborly bonds for isolation and independence. Everyone has experienced feelings of intrusion, obligation, and dependence when kin, a neighbor, or a salesperson drops by for an unexpected visit. If you are in the middle of a project, a nap, or a bath, and the doorbell rings, your first thought may be, "Oh, no, not now. I wonder who it is and what they want." It may be because we lead busier lives that we put a high value on our privacy. It may be because we are more goal-oriented, or it may be because we are more independent and self-resourceful. Whatever the reason, this trend toward isolation is not healthy for some young families because it provides stress, loneliness, and depression. Intimate, supportive relationships, such as kinship or "tight" neighborhoods are important for many reasons. They can provide emergency child care if a parent needs to get away from an emotional scene for a while. They can offer a sympathetic ear to quiet fears to relieve tensions. However, most important, they can provide that outside monitoring system so important for those who need to know someone cares about them and wants the best for their future.

Let us not misunderstand the role of privacy in child abuse and neglect. Privacy alone is not a sufficient factor to produce abuse. Usually several other important conditions are present, such as stress, loss of income, alcohol, loss of a parenting partner, and others. These factors may come together, and if the family is totally isolated from a significant support group, abuse may occur. One might view isolation as the extension of privacy. In a majority of research, the desire for privacy and isolation has been linked to abuse. Many reasons have been given for this linkage. For one, isolation reduces the resources available to the family. It limits their right to call on others for assistance. It discourages a child's contacts for help. Isolation allows unstable, inconsistent parenting patterns to develop and continue. But, most important, it allows early abuse to occur undetected.

Many young families can face job, social, and personal stress and pressure. Many of these families can also work out unstable parenting patterns and practices. Many families can find solutions to the problem of a difficult-to-handle child. They can do all of this. But to do it, they generally need to call on others or get assistance from professionals, kin, neighbors, or friends. Privacy or isolation hinders these families from getting the help they need (Garbarino 1977).

Some countries around the world would weigh the family's right to privacy and the child-protective issue and find the best solution to be total involvement of the State with the mind, thoughts, and life of the individual. In those countries, privacy comes in a poor second. However, in the United States the right to privacy is a heritage. What we must do is keep that freedom and at the same time help our children grow to their fullest potential with freedom from the fear of abuse.

Barrier: Imperfect Screening Tests

Our job of preventing child abuse and neglect would be almost eliminated if we could construct a perfect, never-fail, constitutionally safe screening instrument that could be administered to all prospective parents. If we could identify families who might be potential abusers, we could nip the problem in the bud, or better yet, before the bud developed.

Let us say this test would be given to all parents-to-be three months before the birth of their first child. It could be part of the routine of the regular checkup, like the blood test, the physical exam, and the physician's battery of questions about general health and well-being. This test could have questions to measure self-awareness, self-control, attitudes about child rearing, methods of discipline, and perceived support from and monitoring of kin, neighbors, and friends.

If the results of the test were negative, the parents would be labeled "high risk" or potential abusers. Automatically, the special services and support systems that help abusing parents would be offered or even "mandated" to these newly labeled parents-to-be. Thus, we would have eliminated the problem before it could occur. The perfect answer for prevention? Well, we might have some problems with the acceptance of our questionnaire.

In fact, there are many imperfections in this "potential abuser screening device." Probably the most obvious one is that most parents-to-be would either refuse to answer it or would answer in a way they thought "right" rather than state their true feelings, attitudes, and beliefs. The legally tested concept of *fully informed voluntary* consent is strong enough so that few would willingly volunteer to take such a test once they knew the possible consequences.

But, if you *could* get parents to complete the test, and if you labeled them "potential abusers," would it mold them *toward* abuse rather than away from it? Possibly. Would it lead them to "do as they are called"? Perhaps. There is a strong body of research that suggests that a label (correct or

But, if you *could* get parents to complete the test, and if you labeled them "potential abusers," would it mold them *toward* abuse rather than away from it? Possibly. Would it lead them to "do as they are called"? Perhaps. There is a strong body of research that suggests that a label (correct or incorrect) has an overwhelming capacity to stigmatize. Parents who were labeled as abusers might begin to believe themselves capable of abusing their child and behave in such a way. Consider the negative consequences if the label was false. We might end up with a greater number of incidents of abuse rather than fewer.

But probably the least perfect part of our test to identify families at risk is the unconstitutionality of our method. We have a fundamental constitutional guarantee to the right of privacy in our society. In this age of modern technology, erosions of that right have led to new laws to protect it, such as the Freedom of Information Act.

This act says that unwarranted intrusions on individual rights are denied by law. If, for example, a parent or caretaker has the potential to abuse but has expressed no intent, the state has no right to intervene. Taking it one step further, if an individual actually forms an intent but has not acted, the state still cannot intervene. In most cases, the state takes legal action after the fact, or after a criminal act has been committed (Weisz 1978). So one could conclude that the law is blind to the idea of a parent or caretaker being a "potential abuser."

The powers of the state to intervene or monitor family affairs are stated very clearly in the law. The right to marry and have children is safeguarded by the constitution. Also, the Supreme Court has guaranteed parents the right to rear their children according to their personal values and beliefs. The state does have the power to insist parents provide their children with the basics of food, clothing, shelter, adequate medical care, and education.

If parents fail to provide these things and their child's well-being is threatened, the state may intervene for the child. In cases of child abuse, laws in all fifty states provide for the protection of the child, and the state will intervene if that child is in danger or has been maltreated. But the question is: can a state protect an unborn child from a potentially abusing parent by evaluating responses to a test administered three months before birth? Probably not.

However, many child-abuse authorities believe a screening device is the most promising strategy for preventing abuse. It certainly follows the tried and true preventive-medicine model. Nearly everyone agrees that prenatal checkups help the physician avert potential danger to the health and safety of the mother and the fetus. However, even in the medical arena, preventive screening requires the fully informed, voluntary consent of the patient. The patient must be made aware of the consequences of the screening.

If a screening device such as our Potential Abusers Test were to become routine procedure, parents would have to be told how the test results would be used. They would have to know that no screening instrument exists that perfectly predicts whether parents are potential abusers. If the parents' consent was to be truly voluntary, it couldn't be obtained under the threat to have needed care withheld unless the parent "volunteered." As with any consent form, the parent would have to be told who would hold the information, who would have access to it, and under what circumstances it would be released.

Child-abuse authorities have attempted to construct a screening tool similar to the one we have been discussing. The Michigan Screening Profile of Parenting was developed by a team headed by child abuse specialist Ray Helfer (Schneider, Hoffmeister, Helfer 1976). However, even after screening hundreds of volunteers, the authors stated that the test was not considered a valid instrument, only a research tool or screening instrument. They requested further time for study and research and stated that decisions should not be made about potential abusers on the results of the test. Ray Helfer, specifically, warned against using the screening process itself as a diagnostic test. He emphasized that to separate out a distinct group of parents (or future parents) who might physically abuse or seriously neglect their children will probably never be possible (Helfer 1976).

So our dilemma is quite clear. What we must do is balance protecting children from child abuse on the one hand and on the other hand shield families from invasions of their right to parent. Whether a perfect identifying or screening instrument can ever be developed and implemented is certainly debatable. However, it is clear that if such an instrument ever passes the important qualifying tests, getting parents-to-be to fill it out may be a much more difficult job. Because of the legally tested *fully informed voluntary consent* concept, parents have the right of choice before they act. Some parents would comply, but others definitely would not. Perhaps the hard-to-reach parents who need screening the most would not. So our problem of identifying parents "at risk" is very complex and difficult to solve. Ideas and suggestions for the prevention of child abuse, free of adverse legal implications, will be discussed in following chapters.

Characteristics of Abusive Parents

Once again, the warning must be issued: no one particular set of characteristics fits all abusing parents or caretakers. Parents who abuse or neglect children do not appear unusual. They are not necessarily psychotic or cruel. Abusing parents are usually ordinary people caught up in the complexities of life. Many reasons may exist for their world to reel out of control. Often, child abusers are called "copeless." They are unable to cope with complex problems in their lives. They are often isolated by their own choice and find it difficult to reach out to others for the support and help they need in order to gain control of their lives.

It is impossible and impractical to try to categorize the abusing parent or caretaker. Abuse is found in every category we might define. It cuts across every spectrum of American life, regardless of the color of skin, ethnic background, religious heritage, place of residency, or amount of money earned. Abusers are white, black, brown, yellow, and red. Abusers are atheistic, agnostic, Protestant, Catholic, and Jewish. They live in the wealthiest areas and in the ghettos. They live in city houses and on rural farms. They are white-collar professionals in high-paying, responsible positions; blue-collar workers in menial jobs; and all collar-colors between.

Abusers share only two common characteristics: they abuse their children, and they need and usually want help. However, a few general characteristics seem to occur often in research about abusing parents. These characteristics do not fit all parents, but they tend to combine with others often enough to compel us to take a closer look.

One characteristic already discussed is the preference for privacy that leads to isolation. Abusing parents are isolated from supportive groups such as friends, relatives or kin, neighbors, and community groups. They also consistently fail to keep appointments, discourage social contact, and seldom or never participate in "back-to-school" nights, parent-teacher conferences, or community gatherings.

Another parental characteristic that shows up often in the research is lack of trust. Abusive parents seem to trust no one. Most of them didn't learn to trust others when they were children, and the pattern continues throughout their lives. This inability to trust makes difficult developing relationships. It makes difficult reaching out to others when they are in need. Consequently, the lack of trust combined with preference for privacy and isolation produces loneliness and depression.

A majority of abusing parents were abused or neglected by their own parents. In fact, most research consistently indicates that 85 percent of abusing parents experienced deprivation, if not physical abuse, as children (Elmer 1967). The most consistent feature in the histories of abusive families is the repetition of a pattern of abuse, neglect, parental loss, and deprivation from one generation to the next. This characteristic is also closely linked to a parent's inability to trust. After all, if you can't trust your own parent to comfort you when you hurt, whom can you trust?

Another characteristic common to many abusing parents is unrealistic expectations of their child. They expect and demand behavior that is beyond the child's years or abilities. Probably many reasons exist for these expectations, but one important factor contributes to it more than others: parents do not understand how children grow and develop. They do not understand the stage a child goes through at a particular age. In other words, a parent may try to potty-train a child at one year of age, and yet the child is not physically capable of this complicated task until after age two. The same misunderstanding may be true for self-feeding and all-night sleeping. A basic awareness of what to expect from children is a most important aspect of child-rearing.

Another aspect of this characteristic is that parents may see their child as a fulfillment of their own unmet needs. The parent may ask the child to live up to expectations that a child cannot and should not fulfill. The child may be seen as a source of love or support *for* the parent, instead of a developing personality that needs love and support *from* the parent. The child is perceived as a "miniature adult" capable of adult reason and behavior. If the child fails to live up to this distorted view, the parent may react abusively, particularly if the parent was abused as a child. If the child's actions are viewed as an attack, demanding more than the parent can give, the parent may respond with abuse. The abusive parent would be reacting because of a lack of information or from feelings of inadequacy.

Another characteristic that appears in abusing parents is their belief in harsh punishment for children. They often possess a strong fear of spoiling their child and hold an equally strong belief in the rightness of corporal punishment. You might have heard some parents say, "My old man beat me when I got out of line, and I'm going to do the same thing to my kid! He's not going to get away with anything." Many of these parents believe even babies should not be "given in to" nor allowed "to get away with anything." They need periodically to show their children "who is boss" and to teach respect for authority so that the children will not become too smart or sassy.

Parents who exhibit some of these characteristics often slip into what is called "role reversal" with their children. They create a distorted, twisted relationship. They demand that their children be other than what they can be. If the parents become increasingly frustrated, they may lose control.

Low self-image is another characteristic found in abusing parents. They see themselves as failures, worthless, unable to fulfill the expectations others have had for them. They may be immature and self-centered. Because of these factors they feel they are inadequate parents, incapable of rearing children in an effective, positive way. So they are overcritical of themselves and of their children. They seldom discuss themselves or their children in positive terms. Linked with this characteristic is the fact that they often tend to ignore the child or, on the other hand, they react to him in an aggressive, impatient manner. Observers have stated that little eye contact takes place between these parents and their children. They seldom touch or look at the child, and they ignore his crying. Thus, they seem to lack an understanding of their child's physical, emotional, and psychological needs.

Abusive parents usually go to great lengths to hide their child's injuries. They are reluctant to give information about the child's condition. When they are questioned, they are unable to explain the injuries, or they offer farfetched or contradictory explanations. They respond inappropriately to the seriousness of the child's condition, either by overreacting or by showing little concern or awareness. They may seem more preoccupied with their own problems than those of the child. Often they delay taking the child for medical care—for routine checkups like optometric or dental care or treatment of injury or illness. When they do take an injured child for medical care, they may choose a different hospital or doctor each time (National Center on Child Abuse and Neglect, USDHEW No. [OHD] 76-30099).

The general public's explanation for child abuse and neglect is that the parents are crazy. However, most studies have shown a very low percentage of the total abusing population to be psychotic, psychopathic, or of borderline intelligence. Parents who do exhibit psychotic behavior generally are irrational and extremely inconsistent in the treatment of their children. One moment they are loving and caressing the child, and the next moment they are physically or emotionally abusing him. Parents who seem excessively cruel or act out in sadistic ways can be said to be exhibiting psychopathic behavior. Those of borderline or very low-level intelligence may not be intellectually capable of child-rearing. They may totally neglect the child because they do not know what they are supposed to do. These parents, however, fall into a very small category of the total population of abusing parents.

We may describe many more characteristics that abusing parents possess, but we must remember there is no stereotype. These parents do not fit a single psychological pattern that we can diagnose, diagram, treat, and then prevent. However, many of the characteristics mentioned combine to support and encourage each other with less than positive outcomes. By looking at these characteristics, we have taken one more step toward understanding the complexities of child abuse and neglect.

Characteristics of Abused Children

Characteristics of abused children vary as much as the characteristics of abusive parents. We know from experience or observation that even in the same family, children differ greatly. One child may be quiet, passive, uninterested in events or people; and another may be excitable, hyperactive, boisterous, and aggressive. Just as no two parents are alike, no two children are exactly the same. So it is impossible to try to "characterize" abused children. What we will do is look at some general characteristics that combine to result in abusive behavior.

Although in some cases one child is singled out, it is impossible to predict which child in a family will be abused and for what reason. One child may become the scapegoat for parents and brothers and sisters. He may be the butt of jokes, tricks, and games. No apparent reason exists for that child to be selected, but it happens. In other families, all of the children are abused or neglected.

Often, abuse and neglect start at birth. Sometimes in the first few moments after birth, parents react negatively toward the newborn. Perhaps their baby girl has a hair color or a deformity of a despised relative; or perhaps she simply looks like an average newborn—red, wrinkled, spotted, and fuzzy. If a parent has had expectations other than what they see, they may form a negative opinion that continues through the child-rearing years.

Many factors can enter into the earliest relationships and the bonding period. Consider the mother who was very ill during pregnancy, who had a prolonged and difficult labor and delivery and then an extended recovery. She may think of that child as unusual, different, or bad to have caused her so much trouble. After such a notion has been conceived, it may be reinforced constantly if the baby cries easily, fusses consistently, and is demanding.

This, then, might be one reason for abusive parents: some children, at birth, are seen by one or both parents as unusual or different from their original fantasy.

Some children are very difficult to care for even under the most ideal conditions. Child-care workers have described some of these children as whiny, fussy, listless, chronically crying, demanding, stubborn, resistive, negativistic, pallid, sickly, emaciated, fearful, panicky, and unsmiling (Johnson and Morse 1968).

Any parent of a newborn will acknowledge that care is a twenty-four-hour job. The baby that does not sleep very much, does not cuddle, but arches his back and struggles may tax the most forgiving parents. But the immature, impatient, or disillusioned parent reaches a limit very quickly, and the baby is abused or neglected.

Usually the stress that points up an abusive situation is the infant's crying behavior. Often a father is intolerant of its constant crying and insists his wife take better care of the situation—that she stop the noise so that he can sleep, watch TV, or otherwise be undisturbed. The wife may be doing the best she can with the difficult baby, but her husband's criticism is too much. Her anxiety is reflected in the way she handles the baby. She is tense, jerky, and impatient; the child senses this and cries even more. Eventually, either parent may reach a breaking point and will put a stop to the crying at any cost—by banging the child's head against something or by hitting him or slapping him.

Parents may not realize that crying is the only method their infant has of communicating with them. It is a normal way for a baby to get attention. A baby has different cries for different kinds of attention needed. He may be hungry, anxious, tired, hurting, or simply bored. But unless parents are sensitive to the needs of the child, all the cries sound alike—loud and demanding. The result is that parents have a feeling of helpless frustration. They feel their world is out of control, that they can't do anything about it. Often this feeling leads to rage and striking out.

Some observable signs may identify abused or neglected children, although they are not absolute. Each child's personality is different, and each responds in a different way. But in practical terms, these characteristics should arouse concern, especially when several are present.

To an outside observer, abused children may or may not appear different from other children in physical or emotional makeup; so the identification task is difficult. However, the question is: do the parents perceive their child as "different"? Do they describe him as being "bad," "strange," "unusual," or "weird"? If so, the child may be involved in an abusive situation. Take a closer look.

Does that little boy seem unduly afraid of his parents? Is he fearful of what they will say or do if he is late or has misbehaved in school? Does he often bear welts or bruises? Does he have untreated sores, cuts, or other skin injuries? Do his injuries seem to be inadequately treated? Does he seem to have overall poor care? Is he given food, drink, drugs, or medication inappropriate for his best health and growth? Does he exhibit behavioral extremes? For example, does he cry easily or very little? Does he show no real expectation of being comforted? Is he either very fearful or seemingly fearless of adult authority? Is he unusually aggressive and destructive or extremely passive and withdrawn?

Some children are wary of physical contact, especially when it is initiated by an adult. They become apprehensive when an adult approaches them, particularly if they are crying or acting up. Other children are inappropriately hungry for affection. They may want to reach out but have difficulty relating to children and adults. Perhaps based on their past experience, these children can't risk getting too close to others because they have been hurt too often.

Does that little girl exhibit any sudden changes in behavior? For example, does she display regressive behavior, such as pants-wetting, thumb-sucking, or frequent whining? If she is becoming either disruptive or uncommonly shy and passive, she may be in an abusive situation. In homes where parents are psychotic, disorganized, or chaotic, children are often forced to take the role of the parent. They become protective and attempt to take care of the parents' needs. Does this child evidence any signs of role-reversal behavior?

Does the little boy have a learning problem that cannot be diagnosed? If his IQ and medical tests indicate no abnormalities but he still cannot meet normal expectations, the answer may well be problems in the home—one of which may be abuse or neglect. Particular attention should be given to the child whose attention wanders, who becomes self-absorbed, and who can completely "turn off."

Is the child habitually truant or late to school? Frequent or prolonged absences sometimes result when a parent keeps an injured child at home until the evidence of abuse disappears. In other cases, truancy indicates lack of parental concern or inability to regulate the child's schedule. If the child arrives at school too early or remains after classes rather than return home, as we have said, he might be the victim of neglect.

Again, does the child dress inappropriately for the weather? Children who never have proper coats or shoes in cold weather are usually receiving inadequate care. On the other hand, those who regularly wear long sleeves or high necklines on hot days may be hiding bruises, burns, or other marks of abuse.

These questions point out some general characteristics that abused children share. No one characteristic can account for abuse and neglect. Abused children usually have several of these characteristics in combination.

You might think that when a child becomes school age, surely he would tell someone about his situation. But this is usually not the case. He will not talk about being abused. If he has been reared in an abusive environment, he is suspicious of adults. To him, adults are cruel people who hurt him. In the past they have not offered help, comfort, or joy. Why should he believe that any adult will meet his needs in the future?

Those who work with children should not expect an abused child to seek them out for help. In only the most unusual cases will a child speak out voluntarily.

Strangely, abused children do not usually express hatred toward abusing parents. In fact, a child will often refuse to admit abuse has occurred. He doesn't understand his parent's behavior and often believes the abuse occurred because he did something wrong; he will therefore feel guilty about his supposed misbehavior and will seek love and forgiveness from the abusing parent.

In some instances, children accept their "discipline" as attention from their parents. And, unfortunately, in some homes this is the only type of contact a child has with his parents. So, in a twisted way, he thinks it is better to be noticed by abuse than not to get any attention at all.

It is important that you use care in approaching an abused child. As we discussed earlier, many abused children feel they, rather than their parents, are to blame for the situation or the injury. They are confused and frightened by another adult's concern. They may also fear their parents' retaliation because the injury or incident has been discovered. Sensitive, concerned adults will handle such problems carefully.

Adolescents are just as inclined as younger school-age children to cover up abuse. They think of it as a shameful secret. They are very concerned that no one find out about it because they do not know how to explain it (Kempe, R. and Kempe, C. H. 1978).

Special Problems of the Handicapped Child

Teachers and other adults often do not relate abuse to a handicapped child. But in discussions with teachers, administrators, youth workers, health professionals, and clinicians, a discerning adult can perceive a strong link between them.

We know some parents have unrealistic expectations for their newborn. When that infant fails to live up to that expectation and does not "look" or "behave" in the preconceived way, parents become upset and frustrated and often lose control. We have discussed the: "But I didn't think a child would be so demanding" attitude that first-time parents often express. We also know that some parents see their infant as "different" because of prematurity, low birth weight, or a variety of other factors.

Combining these traumas with a newborn's handicap or multiple handicap can produce serious problems. All parents have adjustments to make to a newborn, but adjusting to a child with cognitive or neurological defects can be an unusually stressful situation. Many times this child's behavior is provocative and unmanageable, causing loving parents to gather every ounce of patience and fortitude in order to cope.

If a parent superimposes lofty, unrealistic expectations on a handicapped child, those expectations will be virtually impossible to fulfill. Often the mentally retarded or neurologically handicapped child serves to reinforce the negative self-image of an abusive-prone parent, causing the parent to feel inadequate, out-of-control, and frustrated so that he lashes out and abuses the child.

We have said that when infants or very young children are battered about the head, tiny blood vessels swell and cause mild forms of brain damage. If that type of abuse continues over a period of time, permanent, severe brain damage can result. So we must ask the question: which comes first, the chicken or the egg? Does the abuse or the handicap come first? Are those children abused because they are handicapped? Or do they become handicapped because they were abused?

Ray Helfer says that authorities agree to the difficulty of determining whether the abuse or the handicap comes first (Soeffling, 1975). They do feel they are closely related. A child who is handicapped, different, or even perceived as different by parents and others is at risk. That child is more likely to be abused by a family that is "abuse prone" than a nonhandicapped child in the same family. Studies of abused children have reported high incidences of retardation, emotional disturbance, physical defects, neurological problems, and growth failure.

Considerable evidence shows that severe physical abuse hampers a child's proper development. However, the most distressing consideration in this link between handicap and abuse is the factor of early maternal deprivation or distorted parent-child interaction. We know that consistent, loving care is essential for infants to grow to their maximum potential. We've learned that children left in their cribs without human attention or affection during the first months of life may die or suffer from a form of retardation. The first year finds a child at a most vulnerable stage of development. If an infant experiences trauma because of abuse or neglect, he can be handicapped for life.

We know now that babies are aware of and understand much more than we ever thought (Brazelton 1979); they are not simply bundles of confusion and noise. A lack of stimulation and positive parental relationships during the crucial early years of life may be one of the greatest handicaps infants are facing.

Parenting begins very early. A growing number of pediatricians, psychologists, and psychiatrists see as crucial a mother's relationship to her baby minutes after birth. The mother-child "bond" develops and continues to grow in those early days and months. Children must be held, cuddled, and touched. However, some normal parental reactions to the birth of a multihandicapped child are rejection, revulsion, shame, and even loathing. Many of these families need counseling by sensitive professionals and lay people who have been through the experience themselves. The guilt feelings accompanying this type of birth are often so severe that even professional counseling has little effect. Caring for a handicapped child is very difficult, yet these children need the same love and attention as those without a handicap.

Finding the balance between neglect and overprotection is difficult. Professionals who work with deaf, blind, and retarded children complain that most of them are either neglected or overprotected by their parents during the early years. Ultimately, these children have to overcome a parenting handicap before they can learn to cope with their physical or mental handicap. Handicapped children with strong, intelligent, supportive parents are more likely to succeed than children who have either overprotective parents or parents who reject them.

Coping with the birth of a multihandicapped child requires the strongest emotional framework possible from parents. The task of caring for that child after birth requires equal stamina, patience, and maturity. Even the best parents of handicapped children need help from trained specialists and understanding from their families and friends. If this help and concern is available when the child is young, the child has a chance to grow and thrive at home and in the community school. Most experts now agree that the child who can remain at home and who receives the help of trained specialists along with equipment and special materials is probably better off than institutionalized children. However, institutions vary, and some provide services that would never be available to handicapped children, especially in rural communities.

Those parents of the handicapped who may be "abuse prone" need special consideration because they are under great stress. Only the best social service programs, sensitive professionals, trained specialists, and concerned lay persons can help these parents cope with their children. Theirs is not an impossible situation. Many children are living success stories; they owe their lives to concerned people who have cared.

Special Problems of the Foster Child

R. H. Mnookin (1974) has provided the following picture of foster child care in our nation:

> There are about 285,000 children under 18 among the nation's nearly 70 million children for whom the state has assumed primary responsibility. These children live in state-sponsored foster care which includes foster family homes, group homes, and child welfare institutions. For a number of the children in foster care, the state has assumed responsibility because no one else is available. Some children are orphans; others have been voluntarily given up by a family no longer willing or able to care for them. A significant number of children, however, are placed in foster care because the state has intervened and coercively removed a child from parental custody. Many foster care placements, perhaps one-half or more, are arranged by state social welfare departments without any court involvement.

The main reasons for placing children in foster care are as follows:
- The physical illness or incapacity of the child-caring person, including her confinement
- Mental illness of the mother
- The child's personality or emotional problem

- Severe neglect or abuse
- "Family problem," including the unwillingness or inability on the part of an adult other than the parent to continue care; children left or deserted, and parental incompetence (Bolton 1978).

The term *foster parent* or *foster home* describes a family or an adult who receives a child for "board and care" from a recognized social agency. Two very important conditions are at the heart of this type of arrangement: 1) the child is placed on a temporary basis, and 2) the social agency may remove that child at any time and cancel the arrangement.

Since maltreatment of children is now one of the leading causes of separation of a child from his family, the establishment of good foster homes and caring foster parents is critical to any community. There can be little argument that this type of separation will leave a lasting impression on a child, no matter what his age or the type of home he may be coming from.

Caring adults hope that the foster care arrangement will be a short-term solution. However, the reality too often is that many children enter this system and for one reason or another do not find their way back to their natural families. They are often confused and unhappy at being removed in the first place and find it difficult to get along with their foster family. Unfortunately, those having the most problems tend to be shifted from family to family. Consequently, many already having a poor self-image begin to think they will never find a person who will understand and care for them.

At best, the foster-care option is less than desirable. However, in many situations the child cannot stay with his natural family or with relatives, and foster care is the only option. The separation must be dealt with as gently and positively as possible, both by the natural parents as well as the foster parents. Yet, this is not always easy, especially on the foster parent. Several factors complicate even the smoothest systems:

- Often the placement agency is vague, evasive, or indirect about how long the child will be in foster care.
- Many times a lack of clarity and consistency exists in the policies of the placement agency.
- The placement agency may caution the foster parents to limit their emotional investment because of frequent changes in child placement.
- Many modern agencies have a case overload and a high turnover of case workers, resulting in a lack of consistent contacts.

These handicaps can cause both sets of parents to feel angry, frustrated, depressed, rejected, and "up-in-the-air."

The needs of the foster child are clear:

- An *environment* that is stable, consistently warm, caring, and loving.
- An *environment* that can adapt to the child's physical, emotional, and social changes.
- *Opportunities* for creative expression, fantasy, imagination, acting-out, and stimulating learning experiences.
- *Adults* who are reliable—who are always there to help meet the child's needs.

The child may have very negative feelings about himself because of the loss of his family and separation from his friends:

- Rejection: "It was my fault."
- Worthlessness: "I don't deserve to be loved."
- Depression: "It will always be this way."
- Anger: "Why did this happen to me?"
- Hostility: "They did this to me."
- Helplessness: "I'm lost. No one will help me."

Usually, several stages occur in any major life adjustment, but these stages are intensified in the foster child's behavior:

- The first one is the *honeymoon stage*. The child (and perhaps the foster parents) believe it is a permanent or semipermanent placement, almost like adoption. Everything appears rosy and wonderful. Everyone is on his best behavior.

■ The second stage is a period of *regression*. The child (and foster parents) begin to have doubts and fears, and the seemingly good progress that was made regresses to a more formal, stiff relationship.

■ The third stage, the *testing behavior*, begins. The child may imply, "If you really loved and cared about me, you'd let me do this or that." These words may actually be spoken.

■ Finally, if the testing behavior is too much for the foster parents, the child is shifted to another family. If not, more positive readjusting is begun, usually more successful in the long run (Bolton 1978).

Trust is basic to the successful adjustment of the foster parents, the natural parents, the child, the social worker, and the placement agency. However, trust is achieved over a long period of time, after everyone involved can communicate freely and a consistent pattern of events and behaviors has been established.

For those who work with foster children who have been maltreated in their natural homes, here are some important facts to remember. Usually the child has experienced a great deal of rejection by his parents. This rejection may manifest itself in two ways: 1) The child has turned to his parents for help and support, and he has been rejected. Since he cannot trust his parents—the people he knows the best and is the closest to—how can he trust strangers? The child builds up a generalized sense of inability to trust others. 2) Along with this inability to trust comes a lack of understanding about why the maltreatment takes place. The child can't remember any specific "wrong" act he did that would cause this type of rejection. Of course, he doesn't believe his parents could be in the wrong; parents are always right. So he begins to believe something about him makes maltreatment appropriate. The overall effect of this reasoning is a feeling of worthlessness and guilt. Foster children thus often come to false conclusions about themselves. Unfortunately, they are masters at covering up their real feelings and emotions. The negative attitudes they have may not be apparent to the foster parents or to others in the child's environment.

The foster child may also have many fears. He may be afraid that one single mistake on his part will have him shifted once again to a place where he is not wanted. He will make mistakes, and it is most important that he is allowed to make mistakes, as everyone should be allowed to do. He must somehow begin to understand that mistakes aren't the end of the world. They do not have to cause major life changes. In addition, his positive behavior must be reinforced, but always with the assurance that he would have been just as well liked and just as valuable if he had less positive behavior. This is a very difficult message to get across to any child, foster or nonfoster (Bolton 1978).

Ultimately, the child must come to believe that he has value simply because he is a human being. This belief requires consistently normal and positive treatment. The last thing the foster child needs is pity from those around him. Pity is an easy emotion; but going that extra mile that might be an inconvenience will be worth the effort for the child's and everyone's future.

Special Problems of the Teen-Aged Parent

The high-risk factor of teen-aged marriages has been given considerable attention lately. The physical, emotional, and social adjustments of these youths are overwhelming to the outsider. Research studies show what many assume: often the reason for teen-aged unions is that the girl is pregnant. Surprisingly little information has been published that assesses their preparation for parenting, their attitudes toward child rearing, and their expectations for their children.

One such report (DeLissovoy 1973) studied a group of adolescent parents over a three-year period, focusing on their parenting attitudes, their knowledge, and their parenting practices. Results showed that young parents went through severe frustrations. They expressed a lack of knowledge and experience, unrealistic expectations of their child's development, and general disappointment with their lives. Generally, their lack of economic resources raised their irritability and lowered their threshold of tolerance.

One of the questionnaires asked the age in weeks, months, or years, at which the parents expected their child to demonstrate certain behavior. Developmental milestones, such as first steps, first words, obedience training, and recognition of wrongdoing, were tested. It was evident that the young parents were not familiar with developmental norms. Consistently the parents said a child should be able to master a task long before the norm indicated. In other words, adolescents thought a child should be capable of certain actions and behavior long before the normally developing child is capable.

Another assessment measured the parents' ideas concerning how often and how long their babies should be expected to cry. Almost one-third of the mothers' responses and almost two-thirds of the fathers' responses suggested an attitude of low tolerance toward their baby's crying.

Another assessment measured disciplining practices and attitudes and the origin of those ideas. Many of the teen parents believed that "doing what comes naturally" would probably be the route they would follow. According to these parents' statements, physical punishment, such as spanking and slapping a child's wrist, hand, or face, were common practices after the child started to crawl. When asked what type of discipline they used to prevent their child from marking on the walls, jumping on furniture, breaking bric-a-brac, and climbing out of the crib, 80 percent of the mothers mentioned physical punishment as their means of control.

In general, the research found young parents to be an intolerant group—impatient, insensitive, irritable, and prone to using physical punishment with their children. In other words, teen-aged parents expected *too much too soon* from their infants and toddlers.

Another research study (Epstein 1979) assessed the attitudes teenagers had before delivery of their child. It reported they had unrealistic ideas of just how much beyond food and diapers their newborn babies would need. The main emphasis of the study was to find out specifically how much the teen-ager knew before delivery about infant development. The basic statement at the conclusion of the study was that pregnant teen-agers expected *too little, too late* from newborn babies. The needs and abilities, especially those related to the cognitive and social growth of infants in the earliest months of life, were greatly underestimated by the adolescents. Basically, they felt the child would be capable of learning or understanding what was going on around him at about two years of age but not much before that time.

The results of this study contrast with the previous study, which stressed the danger of at-risk parents expecting too much too soon from their children. However, almost all of the studies resulting in too-much too-soon philosophies were after-birth assessments. Since the Epstein findings were before-birth assessments, we might make the assumption that teen-agers don't expect newborns to be capable of learning or understanding anything at first, but this notion changes after the birth of the child. In a follow-up study, which is not yet complete, Epstein found preliminary evidence that these same teen-aged mothers did not adequately interact with their children during the first six months after birth. Epstein found the babies were physically well cared for but were neither played with nor talked to by their teen-aged mothers. After all, teen-aged parents might reason, what's the point of playing with babies if they can't understand anything until their second year anyway?

These findings may point up an even larger problem— teen-aged mothers who do not understand the consistent amount of stimulation and nurturing infants need in order to grow and develop to their maximum potential within the first two years of their life.

Another study emanating from the Atlantic Center for Disease Control (McCarthy 1978) studied 2,000 cases of child abuse, including twenty-six deaths. One of the findings was that children born out of wedlock were 2½ times more likely to be abused than children born within wedlock. Out of all the cases involved in the study, 59 percent of the natural mothers had a live birth in their teen-aged years. The concluding statement of this report was "We infer from these data that child abuse may occur less frequently if teen-age childbearing and out-of-wedlock pregnancies occurred less frequently" (McCarthy 1978).

So the question is not whether the harm is in expecting too much too soon or too little too late. Teen-aged mothers need more experience, education, and information to adequately rear and nurture their children. This type of experience may come through age and their own personal maturation process, but if we wait for that to occur, it might be too late to help the child. These facts emphasize that teen-aged mothers are considered at-risk and need our help. If they are put at the center of our concern, their babies will be healthier and happier and better able to reach their fullest potential.

Special Problems of Uniformed Service Families

It is difficult to make generalities about the impact military life has on service families who are abusing their children. For the average layperson, military life is often equated with aggression and violence; therefore, questions are often raised about the relationship of on authoritarian lifestyle in the armed services to childrearing. We might assume that military personnel who lead highly disciplinary lives are apt to be overzealous and punitive toward their children. We might also assume that because military families move a lot, are away from their "monitoring kin," have frequent spouse separations, and lead highly stressful lives, they must have a high rate of abuse and neglect. So the question appears valid: Is child abuse and neglect worse in the uniformed services than in civilian life?

The answer is that no one really knows whether child maltreatment is more or less prevalent in the services than it is in civilian life (Miller 1976). Some theory indicates it might be greater, and even some rudimentary evidence shows it is (Wichlacz et al. 1975). However, equally sound theory and data say abuse and neglect is no more prevalent in the armed services than it is in the civilian community.

Child advocates who are a part of the military scene blame the Department of Defense for not being able to answer the question adequately. They believe the DOD hasn't taken the leadership to provide monies to encourage valid research, facilitate the writing of policies and directives, and design comprehensive treatment programs. The reasons for this are complex, but some say that child abuse and neglect hasn't had the same importance as alcohol and other drug abuse to the national defense position (Miller 1976).

Some unique factors common to military life must be mentioned in order that we may fully understand the total picture. Military life is deeply rooted in bureaucratic organization and a hierarchy of authority. The lines of command are visibly reflected on uniforms, in housing, in job status, and in every aspect of military life. There is never an unemployment problem. The pay is average for those in the average and above-average ranks but can be at poverty level for the low-ranked young marrieds. Provision for medical and dental care is available, as well as other benefits not automatic to civilian families. Some screening takes place before admittance to the military; therefore, supposedly drug abusing, mentally retarded, antisocial, and borderline psychotics would be eliminated at entry. However, no screening program is perfect, and since spouses do not go through the same screening process, the "total health" label can't be applied to all members of military families. Another unique feature is that the commander has responsibility for the total life of the personnel in his charge, and this includes family life.

On the whole, military life has many disadvantages but also enough advantages and benefits to attract and retain personnel. One distinct advantage in terms of child abuse and neglect is the strong sense of belonging to a family or community. Not all military families, particularly spouses, participate in the social life of the military family and so may continue a "loner" pattern established before they joined the uniformed services. Other families live in civilian neighborhoods and choose not to participate in any base benefits and activities. So there are many different types and combinations of military families to consider when asking about their child abuse and neglect status.

Although little research on maltreatment in the armed services suggests any difference between service and nonservice families, some specific stress factors suggest child abuse and neglect could be greater in the military. Those elements that may cause a high-risk family to cross the line from potential status to maltreating status are usually bureaucratic or organizational in nature. Such factors might include a reassignment just when friends have been made and support systems established. Payroll mixups and delays due to the complex payroll system can cause economic stress. A disciplinary infraction or a field-training exercise can take the military family member away from the spouse for extended periods of time. Although none of these factors alone cause child abuse, they can combine to tip the scales until a coping family becomes a family in distress.

Probably the most vulnerable of the military family are the young enlisted members who have just entered or have

been in only a year or two. The same characteristics exist for
these military families as for many young civilian families.
Their lives have elements of immaturity, inexperience, lack
of social skills, impatience, and inability to cope with the
basic problems of life. This is the group most likely to have
the least education and specific life goals. They may be
somewhere between adolescence and adulthood. This is also
the population most likely to have young children.

Two factors complicate the picture: one is that this young
family have recently been removed from their kin, and the
other is that they are the lowest people on the totem pole.
The pecking order is apparent. They do not get the benefits
other military personnel receive. Most of them have to either
make arrangements to move their family at their own
expense to the new location or leave them "back home."
Both solutions put extreme stress on the young family. Low
pay may dictate that the spouse go to work, and then the
problem arises of day care for their child or the solution of
night work, with the spouse babysitting in the evening after
pulling eight to ten hours of duty. However you look at it,
cause for tension and stress is there. But again, all these
events and characteristics can be applied to any young
couple taking a new job in a new area.

If the young military family is at high risk and vulnerable,
it is certainly not the only group in the military with
tendencies toward child abuse; any group with children is
susceptible. However, as with civilian families, the middle-
and upper-middle ranked families have less frequent abuse
records. The reason may be that their children are older, but
it may be also that they can afford to "doctor-select," as
civilian groups do.

As for effective treatment programs, probably the same
elements that work with civilian families work for uniformed
service families. If couples gain maturity, have a desire to
seek help from outsiders, have kin or neighbor support, trust
each other, and have a desire to make their circumstances

work, they generally can cope with the problem of abuse and neglect. The military has social programs, self-help projects, and volunteer clubs to help newly enlisted young families integrate into the military family. It appears that the quicker the adjustment can be made, the fewer incidents of abuse and neglect occur.

However, until the Department of Defense declares war on child abuse from the top down, abuse and neglect will increase. Until data is gathered, definitive programs are established, and specialists are trained, child abuse in service families will continue to be a serious problem that might not effect our military stature abroad, but it certainly will have a great effect on the home-front population.

3
What Is Being Done about Child Abuse and Neglect?

As concerned citizens, neighbors, teachers, and friends, we all have a vital role in the protection of our children. We can demonstrate that we believe our children to be the best resource we have by not allowing abuse and neglect to occur in our homes, schools, or communities. Each individual has a role to play and can be assured that he is backed up in that role by public law.

The Role of the Legal Organization

The Child Abuse Prevention and Treatment Act (Public Law 93-247 [Appendix A]) was signed into law on January 31, 1974. It provided a national focus for the protection of all children in the United States. The new law created the National Center on Child Abuse and Neglect. The Center is housed in the Children's Bureau, Office of Child Development, U.S. Department of Health, Education, and Welfare. This Center has the legal responsibility for administering grants to states and to public and private agencies for programs concerned with child abuse and neglect.

The National Center on Child Abuse and Neglect has developed a many faceted attack on the abuse and neglect problem. First, they continually try to increase awareness of citizens and professionals to the problem and thereby to increase the number of abuse and neglect cases detected and reported. Another goal is to assist states and local communities to develop more effective and efficient mechanisms for the delivery of services to children and families. They are supporting research that will lead to knowledge of the causes of child abuse and neglect as well as to the discontinuation of abusive parental behavior. They continue to encourage self-referrals by parents for help before a crisis occurs. Finally, they hope to provide training and technical assistance to states and local communities to create a concern, a focus, and an increased competence for dealing with the problems of child abuse and neglect.

Whether it be on an awareness level or an action level, agencies, organizations, professionals, and lay persons all should share this multilevel attack. *Someone* must identify the problem and move forward to meet it.

Unfortunately, all too often a tragedy must occur, a child must die under horrible circumstances before anyone recognizes that the problem exists and is able to marshal others to do something about it. As long as this situation prevails, children will suffer and die unnecessarily.

The Law

The Public Law 93-247 defines child abuse and neglect as "physical or mental injury, sexual abuse, negligent treatment or maltreatment of a child under the age of eighteen by a person who is responsible for the child's welfare under circumstances which indicate that the child's health or welfare is harmed or threatened" (see appendix).

Every state requires that suspected child abuse be reported, but every state also defines child abuse and neglect uniquely. Although there are many variations on the theme, most of them are a combination of one or more of the following four elements (Fraser 1978):

- a nonaccidental physical injury
- neglect
- sexual molestation
- emotional abuse (mental injury)

A nonaccidental physical injury may include severe beatings and batterings, human bites, choking or strangulation, burns, or immersion in scalding water.

Neglect is failure to provide a child with the basic necessities of life, such as food, shelter, clothing, and medical and dental care.

Sexual molestation is the exploitation of a child for the sexual gratification of an adult. Sexual abuse includes incest, rape, fondling of the genitals, or exhibitionism.

Emotional abuse is defined as excessive, aggressive, or unreasonable parental behavior that places demands on the child to perform above his capabilities. It can also include inappropriate demands of the child. Some examples of emotional abuse might include constant teasing, belittling, or verbal attacks; insufficient love, support, or guidance (Fraser 1978). Emotional abuse is much more subtle and difficult to isolate and define. It is often found in combination with other abusive and neglectful behavior.

Every citizen should have a clear understanding of his role in reporting suspected cases of child abuse and neglect.

He should know how his state defines child abuse and should be aware of procedures for reporting suspected cases.

Although each state differs somewhat, all states require the reporting of nonaccidental physical injuries. An example of the exact wording in one state defines the abused child as one who "has had physical injury inflicted upon him other than by accidental means" (Fraser 1978). Another state law instructs any physician, hospital intern or resident, county medical examiner, nurse, psychologist, school personnel, social worker, peace officer, or any other person having responsibility for the care of children whose "observation or examination of any minor discloses evidence of injury, sexual molestation, death, abuse or physical neglect which appears to have been inflicted upon such minor by other than accidental means or which is not explained by the available medical history as being accidental in nature" to report to the properly defined agencies (Bolton 1978).

A few states have defined child abuse to include all four elements. The example reads, the abused child is one who "has had physical injury or injuries inflicted upon him other than by accidental means or has injuries which are at variance with the history given of them, or is in a condition which is the result of maltreatment such as, but not limited to, malnutrition, sexual molestation, deprivation of necessities, emotional maltreatment or cruel punishment" (Fraser 1978).

The definitions most states use fall somewhere between these two. A typical example of the middle-of-the-road definition might be as follows: "harm or threatened harm to a child's health or welfare. Harm or threatened harm to a child's health can occur through: nonaccidental physical or mental injury; sexual abuse, or attempted sexual abuse" (Fraser 1978).

Each state, including the District of Columbia, Puerto Rico, and the Virgin Islands, has a mandatory reporting

statute. A copy of this statute can be obtained from one of
these sources:

- A department of social services;
- A law enforcement agency;
- A district attorney's office;
- A city or county attorney's office;
- A state attorney general's office;
- A legislative drafting office; or
- A regional office of Child Development (HEW).

As in any other type of statute, ignorance of the law is not
a legal defense for a failure to report. Every citizen's
responsibility is to obtain and read a copy of his state's
mandatory reporting statute.

The important point to remember is that all states have
child-abuse reporting laws. In some states, fines and
imprisonment are provided for designated individuals who
fail to report. However, most states do provide immunity
from criminal or civil action for people reporting abuse cases.
The main idea is that under state law, you only need to
suspect—not know—that abuse or neglect has occurred in
order to report to the appropriate agency. Then that agency
itself is responsible for conducting an investigation to
determine whether abuse or neglect actually has occurred.

The Legal System

In some child-abuse and neglect cases, the legal system
becomes an integral part of the total picture. The way the
case is handled, in terms of prosecution, punitive action, or
acquittal, is very closely tied to the successful or unsuccessful
treatment and recovery of those individuals involved.
Probably Kempe and Helfer (1972) said it best in their book
Helping the Battered Child and His Family: "Because of the
very nature of the offense and the almost certain danger to
the child, any known cause of apparent child battering
should be brought into the legal process of investigation,
referral to court, and a court proceeding."

They indicate that the quality of the legal process usually determines how effective or ineffective the results will be. Ideally, all parts of the legal system should have one main goal: the best interests of the child and his family. In some situations the first action to reach that goal may be immediate protection of the child from his family. In other situations the family may need to go through a treatment process so that the child can be permanently returned to a well-adjusted, safe home.

However, ideal situations are not always real situations. The legal process for child abuse cases is very complex. If any part of the process breaks down, the system may lose sight of its goal. Breakdowns occur for a variety of reasons: parents become hostile, uncooperative, and fearful because of the way the investigator is handling the case; legal personnel overlook pertinent information or details that affect the case; the attorney or courts are concerned only with the legal aspects of the case; or the proper treatment for the family is superficially designed, implemented, and evaluated. Through these breakdowns, the court system fails not only the child and his family but the community as well.

As we have discussed, most abusive adults and caretakers are normal people who, for many reasons, find themselves out of control. Certainly when we try to imagine ourselves in the shoes of such a parent, we can understand that criminal prosecution in court does not promote or help the emotional growth of the perpetrator. Punitive action certainly does not solve the problem of why the abuse or neglect occurred in the first place. And acquittal may only reinforce the parent's belief that his or her behavior was acceptable when, in fact, it was not.

However, if a rehabilitative treatment plan is established and if agencies cooperate to provide many positive alternatives, the family unit can be saved and the best interests of the child can be protected.

The goal of *adult diversion* directs the parent to rehabilitative treatment. This type of program can be carried out in many different ways. Often a written contract between the parent and the treatment team states specifically and realistically what each person has to do to fulfill his obligation (Bolton 1978).

The types of community resources and their availability can influence a court's decision. For example, a comprehensive, effectively coordinated system allows the court several positive options for treatment. Coordination can be facilitated if a multidisciplinary team can have as its membership representatives from the county attorney's office and the police department.

The *formulation of dispositions*° following a legal judgment can be more meaningful and productive in a multidisciplinary arrangement because of the participation of agencies in the ongoing care of the family and child. The court and team members can make plans for a follow-up review to assess the progress and appropriateness of the original recommendations.

During investigative and court proceedings, the *child counsel* is the child's advocate, promoting the child's rights. In some states such a person is called a law guardian, an appropriate term because this person doesn't prosecute or defend but simply insures that the best interests of the child are protected and preserved. This may be a somewhat unusual role for an attorney, but, indeed, a very important one. If the law guardian has appropriate consultive services, he may and should participate in the disposition planning. His role is a continuing one in which he keeps both the

---

°*Disposition*: the order of a Juvenile or Family Court that determines whether a minor, already found to be a dependent child, should continue in or return to the parental home (and under what kind of supervision), or whether the minor should be placed out-of-home (and in what kind of setting: a relative's home, foster home, or an institution). Disposition in a dependency case parallels sentencing in a criminal case (Bolton 1978).

parents and the social services honest. He insists that the social services provide the agreed-upon services and that the parents take advantage of these services (Bolton 1978).

If the final disposition orders the child to be removed from his home, a great need exists for family rehabilitation and supportive services for the child.

The Law-Enforcement Officer's Role

The dangers involved in a domestic disturbance or family violence are all too familiar to the experienced law-enforcement officer. It has been well documented that almost 20 percent of all peace officers killed in the line of duty were killed responding to some version of a domestic-disturbance call (Bolton 1978). Injuries not resulting in death during response to domestic problems are even more widespread. The child-abuse case is but one more situation that may be placed within the scope of family violence.

Despite the dangers involved, the domestic-disturbance call is a common one in the life of the police officer. It is estimated that in many urban areas 60 percent of all calls coming to police from 4:00 p.m. to midnight are domestic-disturbance situations. Sometimes they are the ones for which the law-enforcement officers are the least trained and equipped to handle.

One of the difficulties in handling domestic disturbances is that the role of the law-enforcement officer is not always clear-cut. People often refuse to press charges against a loved one. The situation may or may not be what it appears to be. The amount of time available to the law-enforcement officer is limited in comparison with the amount of time it usually takes to settle a domestic concern. Yet the law-enforcement officer has a legitimate interest and obligation to protect citizens and enforce laws designed to protect citizens involved in a domestic disturbance.

The key to the law-enforcement officer's role is to bring other members of the service professions into a team that can pool its resources and provide a sound basis in order to aid families in trouble. At no time is this teamwork more important than in the situation involving the maltreatment of children.

Suspected child maltreatment should be reported either to the law-enforcement authority or the Child Protective Services. The majority of these reports are made by telephone. In many states the law mandates that a written report follow up the telephone report, but most agencies agree it is not uncommon to receive the telephoned report only.

In many states three elements in this report are necessary to initiate an investigation: 1) the names and addresses of the minor and his parents or person(s) having custody of the minor, if known; 2) the minor's age and the extent of his injuries or physical neglect, including any evidence of previous injuries or physical neglect; and 3) any other information the reporting person feels might be helpful in establishing the cause of the injury or physical neglect.

Remember, this is the ideal situation. More often, the law-enforcement officer receiving the report will receive only a small portion of the above information. The role of the law-enforcement officer gets even more complex when the decision has to be made whether to receive anonymous reports. However, in almost all states the officer has a legal responsibility to receive an anonymous report and to do his best to follow up on the report with the Child Protective Services. If possible, the law-enforcement agency and the Child Protective Services' office should get together to standardize the screening of reports received by telephone. In this way, both agencies are able to acquire the information necessary to investigate reports. After the report is made, the officer should share it with the Child Protective Services' officer or other members of the support team. This sharing system helps to build the cooperative spirit so that each agency can accept their respective roles with greater efficiency and productivity.

Domestic disturbance and family violence signal danger not only for the family members but for workers and officers who must confront or investigate those persons involved. The set of skills the law-enforcement officer brings to the suspected child maltreatment case should be broad and all-inclusive. If the law-enforcement officer is able to enhance his skills by cooperating with other professionals in related areas, the outcome for the child will be positive and rewarding. The cooperation necessary between law enforcement and social services should always benefit the child and his family.

The Juvenile Court's Role

Every state has a statute allowing some area of the court to intervene in the protection of the child. In most situations this power is given to the juvenile (or "family") court.

The juvenile court, generally, has the right to intervene into the child's life if: (a) a parent or guardian is missing (if the child has been abandoned), (b) if the parent has neglected the child, or (c) if the parent has physically or emotionally injured the child. Juvenile courts across the nation may make specific references to these chldren, such as "persons in need of supervision, dependent persons, or neglected." However, these specific terms may refer to children who are physically injured, emotionally damaged, or in need of some care to insure adequate growth and development. The court may intervene to insure that this care is provided.

The decisions made by the juvenile court are guided by what is termed "in the best interests of the child." The court must then decide on an individual basis what to do. This can be a very difficult task, at best.

The law-enforcement officer's testimony in court may have a significant effect on the life of the child and his family. No position is more powerful than that enabling a court to tell parents they aren't capable of parenting or to separate a child from his family. The responsibility for these decisions cannot be overestimated.

The Child Protective Services' Role

Most states have a child protective services unit within the social services system. The unit may come under a variety of names, but its role is the protection of children and the maintenance of their rights if their rights are being violated.

Specifically, the child protective unit directs services toward families who are having problems with abuse or are showing visible signs of being potentially abusive. They try to prevent dependency, exploitation, and neglect of children by providing social services and programs to help stabilize and preserve the family unit. They provide programs that help parents understand more about child care and child-rearing.

Goals

As a rule, this state agency has specific goals, powers, and duties. Although the duties might be varied, the goals of the child-protection team could probably be summarized by these three processes: 1) *diagnosis*: a determination of whether or not the child has actually been abused; 2) *prognosis*: estimating the probability for successful treatment; and 3) *treatment*; formulating a plan to correct the abusive situation for both parents and child (Roush 1978).

Duties and Powers

The specific duties and powers of most child protective services' personnel include the following:

■ To receive reports of dependent, abused, or abandoned children and to be prepared to provide temporary foster care for such children on a twenty-four-hour basis.

■ To receive from any source oral or written information regarding a child who may be in need of protective services.

■ Upon receipt of such information, to make a prompt and thorough investigation that should include a determination of the nature, extent, and cause of any condition contrary to the child's best interest and obtain the name, age, and condition of other children in the home.

■ To take a child into temporary custody if reasonable grounds exist to indicate that the child is suffering from illness or injury or is in immediate danger from his surroundings and that his removal is necessary.

The child protective services unit has a very high degree of responsibility in the total child-abuse picture. This agency carries out the community's obligation of guaranteeing the rights of children.

Although voluntary social agencies may pull back if the client is unresponsive, the child protective agency must remain active until conditions are improved or the child is protected.

In any abusive situation, intervention is voluntary when the parents initiate the change process themselves, agree to halt the abusive behavior, and desire some type of therapy or treatment program. However, when the criminal and juvenile court systems become involved, voluntary cooperation is usually not successful; intervention then becomes involuntary. The same can be said for the child protective services unit. Its involvement is usually involuntary, and it has the authority to complete the task in whatever way benefits the child in question.

The child protective services team in any community is an expression of the community's recognition that children have basic rights and that parents have obligations and responsibilities. The team protects children when parents, purposefully or otherwise, fail to carry out their primary responsibilities.

The child protective agency holds the authority to protect children through the use of the courts and reserves the right to remove a child from a situation where there is danger to his health, welfare, morals, or emotional well-being.

Other Agencies' Roles in the Community

After a child has been identified as an abused or neglected victim and a prognosis has been made concerning the possibility of successful treatment, a plan with both short- and long-range goals needs to be formulated. At this point, the role of other agencies becomes very clear. The child and his family may need medical care, dental care, day care, mental-health counseling, homemaking services, foster or institutional care, legal or financial services, housing assistance, special education, alcoholism or other drug rehabilitation, vocational counseling or training, and other services. The range of human services must be varied, available, and effectively coordinated.

Community Recognition, Support, and Cooperation

Before we consider the vast array of human services offered to meet the needs of the abused or neglected child and his family, we need to ask some questions. First, *does the community recognize child maltreatment as a problem?* Believe it or not, many communities flatly ignore this problem, fail to recognize it, and look the other way when it occurs. How important the problem is to a community becomes a critical element before one can assess the role agencies other than child protective services and law enforcement can play.

The second question is *what level of support does the community provide for programs attempting to deal with the problem of child abuse?* Support comes in two different packages: one is a financial-support package, and the other is a moral-support package.

In most communities the mandated agency for abuse and neglect is a governmental agency that may or may not receive funds from the state. However, county or local funding is also important in showing a commitment to the abuse problem.

A third question is *how much cooperation is the community willing to give to help the abused child and his family?*

The key element in any program designed to help a certain segment of citizens is broad-based, total community cooperation. The emphasis has to be on a coordinated, comprehensive delivery system that links resources and services together to prevent, identify, and treat child abuse and neglect. Services that can provide this linkage are *health, education, religion, government, agriculture, manufacturing industry, other industry, transportation, economics, social organization, communication, and recreation.* After an understanding is reached regarding the interrelationships of all these areas of the community, cooperation and coordination is no problem.

Comprehensive Emergency Service System

In some communities a comprehensive emergency services system has been the answer to these questions. This system has been defined as a child-welfare service, designed to meet any family crisis or impending crisis that requires social intervention for purposes of planning to protect children whose health, safety, and welfare is endangered, with primary emphasis on those children who will reach the attention of the juvenile court as neglected unless there is immediate casework intervention (National Center on Child Abuse and Neglect, USDHEW No. [OHD] 76-30099).

A comprehensive emergency services system has several characteristics:

- It is a system of coordinated services designed to meet emergency needs of children and families in crisis.
- It provides options in care that will protect children and reduce trauma induced by the crisis.
- It provides a vehicle for cooperative program planning.
- It provides quality service on a twenty-four-hour basis, including weekends and holidays.
- It emphasizes maintaining children in their own homes whenever possible rather than separating them from their home environment.
- It seeks to provide services to children and their families when it is necessary to separate children from their home environment in a more orderly, less damaging way (National Center on Child Abuse and Neglect, USDHEW No. [OHD] 76-30099).

And the following components are basic to a comprehensive emergency service system:

- Emergency intake
- Outreach and follow-up
- Emergency neighborhood crisis centers
- Emergency shelters for families
- Emergency caretakers
- Emergency homemakers
- Emergency foster family homes
- Emergency shelter for adolescents

(National Center on Child Abuse and Neglect, USDHEW No. [OHD] 76-30099).

These components must mesh into a cooperative network of services to prevent a child from being placed in a bureaucratic cycle that can be more damaging than the crisis itself. If the comprehensive emergency service system is well coordinated, it can provide options as well as reduce trauma caused by a crisis in a family.

Most communities have discovered that a coordinating committee is essential to insure the success of a comprehensive emergency services program. Any concerned citizen can start the impetus toward forming a committee. Membership in the committee needs to be wide and varied. Because child protective services and law enforcement are usually the mandated agencies to serve abused and neglected children, their representatives are necessary and valuable members of the coordinating committee.

Other members of the committee should include representatives from the juvenile court, the county attorney's office, and, if applicable, the attorney general's office. These public agencies must rely on the total community for referral, treatment, preventive resources, advice, and consultation (Steiner 1978). The purpose of the committee is to allow maximum utilization of the total community as a resource.

Other members of the committee should include representatives from public and private schools, health and mental-health services, local government, churches, shelter-care facilities, day care, citizen groups, and other community groups.

Some important qualities and characteristics members of the committee need to have are credibility in the community, motivation to improve services to children and families, political clout, and capability of impact so that the committee has the community's support and sanction to effect change (Steiner 1978).

Some of the basic tasks the committee should consider are these (Steiner 1978):

■ To assess whether the community recognizes maltreatment as a problem. Since no community is immune from incidents of child abuse and neglect, the community must assume an attitude toward it and a community desire to do something about it. If not, education and awareness of the problem may be the committee's first action.

■ To assess existing community resources, services, and needs. Every community has its strengths as well as its weaknesses. The community needs to capitalize on their

strengths and remember that citizens are the greatest
resource of the community.

▪ To establish a common philosophy and define long- and
short-range goals.

▪ To obtain a commitment from the group to work together;
to offer ongoing suggestions; to develop mutual trust, respect
and appreciation; and to clarify realistic expectations, goals,
and objectives.

▪ To set some guidelines for evaluating how effective the
committee is in accomplishing the tasks decided upon and
evaluating the coordination of services to the abused child
and his family.

Barriers to Coordination of Services

Coordination and linkages of service agencies has not
always been a smooth and easy task. Because of some of its
pitfalls and difficulties, interested persons must pay attention
to the inherent problems involved.

In many communities, despite continued efforts to
improve interagency communication to deal with child
rights, progress toward improved relationships remains poor.
At times the child and the family get lost in the bureaucratic
shuffle between agencies. Moreover, incredible duplications
of services occur, leaving the family confused and frustrated.

In some rural areas, follow-up and long-term
rehabilitative services for families in trouble are minimal at
best. This shortcoming applies also to some urban
communities. In many areas preventive education and
services are either nonexistent or inadequate. Some
communities have "invisible" treatment programs scattered
throughout a variety of local human service agencies,
educational institutions, and community groups. Without
coordination of existing services, the family may find it not
worth the time and effort required to seek them out. Too
often when a child-abuse and neglect case is brought to the
attention of an appropriate service-provider, administrative

problems and mixups can foil the actual delivery of services. Because a complex combination of services is needed to restore the well-being of a family, supercoordination and service delivery must be accomplished to make it work. Too often red tape, inflexible funding requirements, and buckpassing deal service delivery a slow and painful death.

Why is service-coordination so hard to accomplish? One reason is the law the federal government passed to mandate reporting of child abuse and neglect. In some states the number of cases reported has increased by 500 percent, and yet the service agencies still operate with the same number of personnel as before the federal law went into effect. The distressing fact is that even with a 500-percent increase, the number reported is still only a fraction of the actual children estimated to be abused and neglected. So the issue is that the problem is much bigger than the equipment, the facilities, and the staff agencies have to handle it.

We know that some doctors still send children home from the hospital without being sure that the injuries they treated were accidental and not inflicted. We also know that some teachers still feel they should "mind their own business" rather than report a pupil believed to be abused or at risk. The tip of the "reporting iceberg" can barely be seen. No federal laws exist to bring about the basic remedy needed most—concern and coordination at the community, the state, and federal levels.

In areas where coordination is working more successfully than others, the key seems to be a community liaison group or central coordinating committee. This committee provides a forum for differing philosophies or points of view on the assessment, treatment, and direct service plan to be developed and carried out for the child and his family.

A look toward the future suggests more and more cooperation will be needed to get the job done. However, when concerned professionals and lay persons put their heads together about the problems of coordination of services, institutionalization of youth, and more successful programs to meet the needs of the abused child and his family, the following recommendations usually surface as agreed-upon goals for the future:

- Wherever possible, children should be treated in their own homes.
- If children must be removed from their homes to prevent harm to them, they should be placed in a homelike setting, such as a foster home or a group home in their community.
- Child services should be offered by private, competing agencies, not by the government, and should be answerable to the residents of the communities where they are located.
- Instead of direct financing of institutions, which encourages their holding on to children, a voucher system should be used that moves the money with the child.
- A large education program should begin to convince parents, neighbors, and volunteers that day care, group homes, and halfway houses are needed in communities.
- Standard rights and advocacy programs should be established for all children in all institutions.
- Children should not be punished for refusing treatment, and they should be required to do only what is required of all children, such as mandatory education.
- Construction of large hospitals for the mentally retarded, prisons, and detention centers should be halted.
- Existing large institutions should be replaced by smaller institutions near large cities.
- Institutions should have no more than twenty beds, and there should be one staff member for every three children.
- Mentally retarded children should never be placed in institutions.
- Juveniles should be locked up only for violent crimes—rape, murder, bombing, arson, and serious assaults—but never for misbehavior or "status offenses," like runaways or truancy that would not be punishable if committed by adults.

- Staff in institutions should be trained to be watchdogs for children's rights.
- Restraints, such as corporal punishment, drugs, and isolation, should be replaced by the use of crisis intervention teams.
- Institutions should be monitored by an independent agency with powers to investigate complaints and conduct public hearings. Complaints about abuse also should be reported to parents and police (Titus 1977).

So although progress has been made, we still have a long way to go in meeting the needs of the abused and neglected child and his family. The basic action needed is a better understanding of the abuse problem and closer coordination to provide the wide range of services needed by the family. This action must emerge and grow at all levels—local, state, and federal. It is just as important that federal and state agencies understand and coordinate as it is for the grassroots community organizations. This action will reap positive results for the child, his family, and all of society.

The Special Role of Educators

Educators and others who work directly with children in the schools have an excellent opportunity and a grave responsibility to identify and report suspected cases of child abuse and neglect. Authorities agree that the classroom teacher, particularly, should become the most important link in the preventive and protective chain. Because of daily contacts with the child, the teacher is in a strategic position to observe early indications of abuse.

In order to be effective, teachers, principals, school nurses, aides, custodians, food service personnel, and other school system employees must seek information and education about the problem of child abuse, about their state's legal requirements and provisions, about local reporting procedures, about their school policy, about the symptoms that indicate a child may suffer abuse or neglect, and about how they can assist the abusing parent.

Educators have a long record of caring, listening, and responding to children and families under stress. This record should produce a sense of leadership and influence among today's educators. Unfortunately, with the current concern over individual rights, litigation against professionals, and increasing alienation of individuals within our society, the role of the educator is moving away from involvement with the family. Human loss is occurring because individuals and institutions are moving from a position of active personal involvement to one of instructional process as a primary goal.

However, teachers still have a personal and weighty influence on the lives of children. Principals remain disciplinarians, and children respect them. The staff of the cafeteria or maintenance units are still the friendly, academically uninvolved, caring people to whom children respond and with whom they enjoy interacting during the school day.

Educators' Responsibilities

Educators and other school personnel thus can play a vital role in preventing child abuse, partly because they have almost daily contact with children above the age of five. More importantly, they have the skills, the ability, and the experience needed to identify unusual physical conditions and out-of-the-ordinary emotional behavior.

Sometimes educators point out that most abuse concerns preschoolers; therefore, they do not have to be concerned. The statistics show that while the more severe cases of physical injury resulting from abuse tend to involve preschool children, particularly infants, the incidence of maltreatment among children aged five through eighteen is significant. Estimates from 30 to 50 percent of all incidents of physical abuse occur within the five- to eighteen-year age span. Injuries incurred by school-aged children are often bruises resulting from spankings, whippings, and lashings with a belt or cord. If the marks can't be covered with clothing, the child may be kept home from school until the evidence fades.

Some of the evidence suggests that the plight of the school-aged child has been pushed into the background by the visibility of that of the preschool child. The helplessness aspect of the infant and toddler may overshadow the maltreatment of the school-aged child.

However, the question is not one of reason or of age; all children need the positive support and help of the educator. The first role of the adult educator in the child maltreatment situation is to care. It may sound like an oversimplification of a complex problem, but the effective intervention in the life of an abused child takes time, patience, commitment, consistency, and many other virtues in the "beyond the call of duty" category. The abused child may be an extra burden to the educator because he is always underfoot. The maltreated child will demand time to express fears, concerns, hopes, and sorrows. It may be a long, difficult, unending task. Because the child has been hurt by an adult, he will test and try a relationship to see if he can trust it.

In today's world of transient living styles, lack of extended family or kin support systems, and single parents, the child may turn to the educator as a temporary representative of the kind of person he wants to have as a parent. The educator may become a "psychological" parent. He may provide that continuing, day-to-day companionship, give-and-take, and compassion so needed by the child to fulfill both his psychological and physical needs (Bolton 1978).

While all parents face some conflict in raising their children, most parents can cope with problems and come to terms with decisions that have to be made. However, some parents are subjected to a level of stress that causes a family breakdown and manifests violent acts.

Some of these acts have signs or warning signals that appear and can be "read" or observed by the educator. None of these signs will *always* precede a violent act but can combine with others to warn the alert educator. Generally the educator may observe the following behavior:

- Children who say or demonstrate they can't communicate with their parents.
- Families whose members seem to have little or no reciprocal relationship.
- Parents who complain that their child is a burden, is destructive, or is somehow "bad."
- Inadequate child care by the parent accompanied by the firm notion that they are competent to undertake the task and are doing a good job of it.
- Overly restrictive attitudes, or just the opposite, overly permissive attitudes.
- Children who are unable to demonstrate or communicate their needs to other adults out of fear or passive resignation that it will do no good.

Again, it is critical that the educator avoid falling into the trap of assuming that the outside view of the family is the real view. The alert, responsible, skilled educator can identify the child with emotional and psychological problems. Then, over a period of time, the educator can question the child and obtain other information that will give the true picture of the situation.

Child-abuse experts caution educators to avoid some approaches in dealing with the abused and neglected child. For example, if a teacher questions harshly or too specifically about the child's injuries, he will state he "fell" or "accidentally burned" himself rather than say his parent harmed him. Teachers should avoid making derogatory or disparaging remarks about parents—even if it appears the parents have abused their child. Teachers should not contact parents on their initiative to "get to the bottom" of the problem.

Sometimes an educator will suspect the presence of child abuse and neglect but will be uncertain of the diagnosis. One of the better ways to handle this situation is to talk with the child in a private setting. Another method is to contact the person in most schools who has the greatest experience with injuries—the school nurse. Nurses can usually look at a child and make the decision as to whether the injuries are accidental or inflicted. Occasionally it is wise to obtain a telephone consultation with a pediatrician who is a trauma expert. Some pediatricians will be willing to offer an opinion over the telephone if they receive specific descriptions.

After the diagnosis is certain, the educator should have no question as to the best course of action. Until abuse and neglect problems are dealt with, the child is usually too entrapped by them to concentrate on his school work; so the sooner the educator reports his findings, the better it will be for everyone involved.

Educators' Legal Status

Usually the legal role of the educator ends with the identification and reporting process. However, his involvement with the case will continue because probably no other person besides the child's parents has such prolonged, consistent access to the child. This type of observation can be valuable for planning further treatment for the child and the family.

The possibility exists that a teacher may be involved in the intervention process. However, unless he actually sees the child being abused, he probably won't be asked to testify or to appear as a witness in court. Persons who have seen the evidence of bruises or burns cannot offer an opinion because they can testify only that on a certain date a child appeared at school with certain injuries. They don't have firsthand knowledge of how those injuries were inflicted. The same testimony can be given by the physician, although his words are valued as an "expert witness" instead of a "lay witness."

Because of the fear of personal liability, many educators hesitate to report suspected child abuse and neglect. As in other criminal reporting, educators fear that if the charge is in error, the parents will sue them. However, if the report is made in good faith, there is no chance that such a suit would be successful. Although statistics are difficult to obtain, several child-abuse authorities have stated that to the best of their knowledge no one in the United States has ever been sued for reporting in good faith. Good faith simply means an honest belief by the reporter that the child was being abused or neglected.

Every state has some form of immunity from civil and criminal liability; so the reporting person is protected. The idea is to identify the child at the earliest possible moment. Once a child is identified, the investigation can begin. If an educator says, "It's none of my business"; "I don't want to get involved"; or "Let someone else do it," he is forgetting that child abuse is going to recur because it is a patterned behavior. In many states, an educator or other professional who is mandated to report abuse and willfully does not is breaking the law. So a conscious decision not to report may lead to further abuse and can result in personal liability on the "other side of the fence" (Fraser 1978).

In other words, an educator who is negligent in performing his duties may be liable. However, the main point still stands: educators who are caring, committed, and concerned about the welfare of their students will fulfill their professional and moral obligations. They will report suspected cases of child abuse and neglect so that the earliest possible help can reach the child.

The Child Abuse Liaison System

In some states a special educator is designated as a school liaison specifically to handle abuse and neglect issues. This person may act as a go-between, an awareness educator, a consultant, a listener, a written-policy maker, or a combination of all of these. In some instances the liaison cooperates with the protective services staff as a team member involved in evaluating the case and developing a treatment program for the child and family. Since the school is an excellent place to observe the effects of the investigation on the child, the liaison can be an important member of the team. The school is one of the first social agencies to see whether the abuse is continuing.

Another important task that the liaison can perform is inservice training programs for educators, staff, and parents. These programs should include the rights and responsibilities under the law, identification and dynamics of child abuse and neglect, and school policy and procedure. Areas to cover in such training sessions would be the attitudes and values school personnel hold toward family privacy, corporal punishment, and the rights of children. Successful programs show that comprehensive inservice training for all school personnel, including board members, increases the effectiveness of the school-policy involvement level and the number of cases reported.

Written Policies and Procedures

The educator's hesitation to identify and report child abuse can partially be eliminated by a clearly written, easily understood school policy. A policy regarding child abuse and neglect is a commitment by the school to cooperate with other agencies and professions. It suggests that the school is aware of the problem and wants to help in identification, investigation, and treatment or preventive problems.

The following items might be included in such a policy:
■ A specific definition of the abused and neglected child as stated by law.
■ A statement that educators and other school personnel are mandated by law to report suspected abuse and neglect incidents and a rationale for their being so mandated.

- Instruction to educators about their legal obligations and immunities in regard to reporting.
- The name and appropriate section numbers of the state reporting statute.
- A list of the persons or agencies to whom the reports are to be made.
- A statement of the type of facts required of the person reporting.
- A statement of how the person is to report, whether by telephone followed by a written report, or by written form only.
- If one schoolperson is responsible in a liaison position, that person's name, his phone number, and a brief description of his duties.
- Examples of properly completed state or school reporting forms with instructions to destroy the form should the report be unfounded.
- Policy concerning interviewing students at school.
- A statement concerning the availability of school health personnel.
- A note concerning the access to a camera for photography and a method for referral to local clinics or hospitals for examination and photographs.

After a policy has been developed and refined, it should be approved by the local board of education, the school board, the parent group, and the teachers and administrators. The key to good cooperation and effective coordination is wide dissemination of the policy. The news media might be a good place to start. Radio, television, and newspaper stories announcing the formulation of an all-school philosophy and policy may be the first step toward preventing acts of abuse and neglect.

The policy must be reviewed and presented each year not only for new staff but also as a reminder for continuing personnel. Some type of ongoing training in abuse and neglect should also be a part of the inservice program at the beginning of each new school year.

Child abuse and neglect are common problems in our society. Educators and other school personnel are in a strategic position to identify it early. After they have uncovered a suspected case, they should immediately report it to the liaison or the child protection agency for evaluation and treatment. This intervention is critical because it can break the vicious cycle of children growing up to become tomorrow's child abusers and violent members of our own society. In all instances it will help a child better realize his educational potential. In some instances it may help save a child's life.

4
What Can I Do about Child Abuse and Neglect?

Everyone has a role in fighting the battle against child abuse and neglect. Everyone also has a grave responsibility to take some steps toward action. Why? Because everyone is an observer. we live in neighborhoods, work at jobs, shop in communities, attend churches, lead youth groups, go to schools, play in parks, attend ball games, and participate in groups and organizations. Because we are in daily contact with children and families, we are primary sources of information about the child-abuse problem.

Our job is not to investigate suspected child abuse and neglect; investigation, diagnosis, and prognosis is the responsibility of a state agency specifically designed for that purpose. Our obligation usually ends with reporting our observations and suspicions.

Why, then, are we not doing our best to fight abuse and neglect? Surely we believe our children are worth the effort. One answer may be that the basic attitude people have about abuse and neglect is a hands-off one. That attitude must be changed. Let us look at some basic steps that can be taken to fight abuse and neglect.

You Can Fight Community Attitudes

One way to do something about child abuse and neglect is to fight existing community attitudes about the problem. Because of stories on television and radio and in newspapers and magazines, most Americans are aware that children are abused and neglected in their state, their city, and perhaps even their community. However, when they are quizzed about abuse and neglect in their own neighborhood, they demonstrate that their awareness of abuse "somewhere" and their acceptance of their responsibility for it are two different things.

Common Statements Reflecting Attitudes

People in a community say, "It can't happen in my neighborhood! Why, everyone is so nice. Most families are church-going, and they do things together. It probably happens in other areas, but there's no abuse and neglect on Cherry Street!"

A similar comment may be something like this: "It's *those* people who do it. They're a little crazy and unstable. They're the ones who would abuse and neglect their children."

Another community attitude is reflected in this statement, "Middle- and upper-income parents never maltreat their children."

People who want to look the other way say, "I'm glad I don't have to worry about the problem. Doctors and hospitals take care of it."

Those in the community who believe strongly in the biologic ability to parent will say, "As long as a mother is in the home, the child's normal development is guaranteed."

A survey by David Gil in 1970 revealed that although most American adults were aware of the existence of child abuse and neglect, only 3 percent of American adults had personal knowledge during the course of a year about families who physically injured a child. One can only hope that a decade later people are talking more openly about their needs and seeking help more readily for their problems.

When protecting children and stabilizing families is the issue, the fight against community attitudes must be declared as a war on myths, misconceptions, prejudices, apathy, and a general lack of concern.

You Can Understand the Effects on Children

When you really begin to understand the long- and short-term effects on children of child abuse and neglect, it is very hard for you to look the other way or to ignore the problem.

Long-Term Effects of Abuse and Neglect

Severe physical abuse of a young child almost always results in difficulties in later development. Studies of abused children have reported a high incidence of long-range mental retardation, physical retardation, brain damage, learning disabilities, physical defects, neurologic problems, psychological problems, and growth failure. Some studies have found a significant difference between abused and nonabused children on both verbal and IQ measures. Abused and neglected children score lower than nonabused children (Sandgrund, Gaines and Green 1974).

In 1974 H. P. Martin and others followed up on the condition of abused children four to five years after the physical injury. They reported that a large group of them had neurological handicaps, ranging from serious to mild. Another large group exhibited growth failure and symptoms of failure to thrive. (As we have said, "failure to thrive" is a diagnostic category of infants who are subjected to severe malnutrition, resulting in developmental lags. They are often irritable and apathetic and have poor eating habits; they may vomit a lot and have diarrhea.) Children can die from the failure-to-thrive syndrome, but more often brain damage is the long-term result of this early problem. Martin et al. (1974) concluded that:

> While the amount of data is small, it is clear that the abused child is at high risk for damage to his nervous system and maldevelopment of ego functions. Actual loss of central nervous-system tissue by physical trauma accounts for the mortality and much morbidity in these children. However, more subtle effects of the environment that may be associated with the abusive home are beginning to be recognized. The abusive environment, apart from the actual physical trauma, impairs the development of the child neurologically, cognitively, and emotionally.

Evidence of earlier abuse or continued abuse shows up in classrooms, in youth groups, and in neighborhoods. These children seem to be unable to enjoy life, and they tend to withdraw from normal social relationships. Abused and neglected children fall behind their peers in toilet training, motor skill development, socialization, and language development. And, as the statistics seem to agree, if the pattern of abuse is allowed to continue, abused and neglected children become abusive and neglectful parents.

Because the personal dignity of these children has been assaulted, their sense of self-worth has been obliterated. Many abused children carry a poor self-image for the remainder of their lives. Little doubt exists that the long-term results of early or continued abuse and neglect are crippling and faulting for life.

Short-Term Effects of Abuse and Neglect

The short-term effects of physical abuse are usually obvious bruises, scars, broken bones, broken teeth, abrasions, cuts, and even death. Short-term injuries may heal quickly, but the real damage is an internalization process that shows up later as the child is measured against his peers.

Unless these children receive adequate treatment, they will not develop the social, psychological, intellectual, and emotional skills needed to be happy, healthy, productive members of our society.

Need for Long-Term Programs for Abused and Neglected Children

Unfortunately, many programs treating *parents* overlook the *children* who need long-term treatment, also. Those children whose parents never developed nurturing abilities even after extensive therapy may still be hurting. Sometimes, therapy for abusive parents results in no detectable changes in the parent-child interaction even after treatment over an extended time. The child may no longer be battered in the technical and legal sense, but he may still be experiencing hostile rejection and excessive physical punishment. Long-term programs for abused and neglected children must be improved. However, as we have said, the needs of these children may be ignored because of an emphasis on child-abuse programs treating parents.

Another point must be made. An abused child's problems will not necessarily disappear because their parents successfully respond to treatment. The damage may be so severe that the child will never fully recover. Abused children need therapy, too, both short- and long-term.

You Can Know How, Where, and When
to Report Child Abuse and Neglect

When smoke is pouring out of a building, when cars
screech and suddenly collide, when a masked gunman races
out of a building, when someone collapses on the sidewalk,
we know where to call for the appropriate kind of help. We
usually feel pretty confident about doing so, even if it occurs
outside normal working hours. However, if a two-year-old
child is covered with bruises or burns, the average neighbor
or relative is completely at a loss. Even most professionals
(doctors, educators) coming in contact with the child are not
aware of the procedures to follow. Almost everyone wonders
about the risk of getting involved and the liability
possibilities.

Even when the appropriate designated agency is well
known, it may enjoy so little of the public's confidence, for
one reason or another, that people fail to act. They fear that
reporting would be useless. And at times the child's situation
is not seen as an "emergency"; so no one moves to help.

Much of our inability to help suffering children stems
from confusion about the laws and the procedures of
reporting. Some of the basic questions must be settled in
order for the identification, investigation, and intervention
process to be complete.

Who Reports?
The question of who reports is easy to answer: *everyone.*
Every state has a reporting statute listing a profession or
group of professions that must report when they have
reasonable cause to believe a child has been abused. States
revise and amend these statutes continuously, but the overall
trend has been toward expanding the classes of persons
required to report. Although some people have a legal
mandate to report, that does not mean the average citizen or

neighbor is off the hook. *Everyone* can report and should feel a moral obligation to do so.

Since the first step toward solving the problem is locating and reporting cases of child abuse, the reporting stage is critical to the welfare of the child and his family. Abusing parents will seldom reach out for help; so one of the most effective ways to move the child and his family toward help is to begin the process of identification.

What Do I Report?

Knowing what to report and knowing how to determine abuse and neglect can be helped by your asking some very simple questions:

First, look at the child's *appearance.*

- Does the child have bruises and burns? Cuts and scratches?
- Is the child consistently unwashed, with sores on his arms and legs?
- Does the child have patches of missing hair?
- Does the child look thin, emaciated and underfed?
- Is he dressed inadequately for the weather?
- Are the child's articles of clothing, particularly his shoes, too big or too little?

By themselves, these questions aren't reliable indicators of abuse and neglect. In fact, any one of these questions could be answered in the affirmative for just about any normal child under normal conditions. However, if the child usually has this appearance, or if a pattern occurs, the child may be at least neglected and probably is being abused.

Second, look at the child's *behavior.*

- Does he consistently complain of hunger or missing meals because of punishment?
- Does he linger at neighbors' homes at mealtime, hinting for an invitation?
- Does he tend to be either extremely fearful or overly compliant?

- Does he cry constantly?
- Does he frequently miss school?
- Does he appear to be largely unsupervised? Is he left unattended for long periods of time? Is he seen wandering about the neighborhood at unusual hours?
- Does he go to great lengths to avoid confrontation that might lead to further abuse?
- Is he forced to take over adult responsibility for long period of time?
- Is he overworked? Exploited? Exposed to unhealthy conditions in the home?
- Does he exhibit emotional problems or severe illnesses that the parents fail to care for or treat?
- Is he demanding, aggressive, and angry due to continual frustration?

If the answer to several of these questions is yes, and if the behavior is consistently exhibited over a period of time, you have good reason to suspect the child is being abused or neglected.

Where Do I Report?

Every state has at least one agency to receive reports of suspected child abuse and neglect. In most states the agency is called the Department of Social Services. In some states it is called the Department of Youth and Family Services, the Department of Social and Rehabilitative Services, or the Department of Child Protective Services.

In some states more than one agency is mandated to receive suspected reports of child abuse, resulting in some confusion. Of course, the best place to report is the agency that can respond immediately and will conduct a concerned, nonthreatening, nonpunitive investigation. In most states this agency is usually the Department of Social Services.

When Do I Report?

Every state requires that a report of suspected child abuse be made "immediately" or "promptly." In other words, this means people are obligated to inform the appropriate agency the moment they suspect abuse.

How Do I Report?

Many states require simply that an oral report be made, and that can be done by telephone. A few states require that a written report follow the oral report. A number of states now provide a twenty-four-hour toll-free telephone number for reporting suspected child abuse. Look in your telephone directory for any of the agencies listed above.

How Sure Must I Be Before I Report?

No fixed rule indicates what is sufficient evidence for reporting. The terms used in state statutes are "reasonable cause to believe" and "reasonable cause to suspect," and they are very difficult to define. Common sense and moral obligation solve the problem by ordering, "If doubt exists, resolve the doubt in favor of the child, and report."

Following are other questions that might be useful in deciding whether to report child abuse:

Must I Identify Myself When I Report?

The answer is no, but it is better for the child and the agency if you do identify yourself. If follow-up to the report is needed, you are available. If the agency needs information that has been omitted, they can ask for it.

Do I Have Legal Protection When I Report?

The answer is yes. Persons who report *in good faith* are granted immunity from civil and criminal court action, even if the report proves to be erroneous. Many people fear that if they identify themselves when they report a suspected case of child abuse, the child's parents will sue them if it is erroneous. The fact is that every state has a child abuse law or statute granting immunity from civil and criminal liability if the report of suspected child abuse has been made in good faith (Frazer, 1975). To reassure yourself of your legal protection, read the exact wording of your state's child-abuse law.

What Happens After I Report?

As the telephone call or written report is received, the intake process begins. The receiver decides three issues:

■ Is this the appropriate agency? If not, the caller is referred to the proper agency.

■ How serious is the reported incident? Is the child's life or health in danger? If so, an immediate investigation must be made.

■ Which person on the staff is the most appropriate one to handle this case?

After a caseworker has the assignment, he has the responsibility to conduct a thorough investigation. The investigation should take a close look at the child's life, not just at one injury or incident. Since child abuse is a pattern of behavior, a proper investigation has to look at the total picture of the child and his family from birth to the present time.

In most physical- and sexual-abuse cases, the caseworker gets the child to a licensed physician as soon as possible. If it is a physical abuse case, the physician records each identifiable injury according to the type, extent, location, severity, and length of time it has been there. After a physician conducts an extensive examination, his responsibility is to determine if the injuries are consistent with the explanations the parents have given for their occurrence, and he determines whether the injuries are the result of accidental or inflicted action.

Interviews take place between the caseworker and the child, the parents, other family members, the child's teacher, perhaps neighbors, and the person who has made the report. The caseworker will also check to see if any other reports exist involving this family.

When the results of the examination, the interviews, and other data have been gathered and the investigative part of the process is finished, the caseworker must decide several things:

- If this is a case of child abuse, do the injuries, or does the behavior of the parents fit the state's definition of child abuse?
- Will a treatment program for the child and his parents be successful?
- Of the variety of treatment programs, which will be the most effective in order to help the family to wholeness?

The investigator must make the basic decisions as to what actions may be best for the child. If, upon receiving the original report, the investigator decides the family is in crisis and the child's life is in danger, the child may be immediately removed from the home. An evaluation may have to be made on the spot, followed later by a thorough investigation. The investigator is the middle-person who ties together the original suspicions and the final treatment of the problem. The entire case depends on the data that is gathered.

After the data is gathered and analyzed and decisions have been made about the family's willingness to cooperate, the treatment program begins. In most child abuse cases a voluntary agreement takes place between the child's parents and the local Department of Social Services. This type of intervention, as I explained earlier, is called *voluntary intervention*. It occurs when the family is willing to try to solve their problem and indicates they are anxious to cooperate. They must not have had other reports of abuse, and the child's injuries should not be severe. The caseworker monitors the treatment process and notes the progress the family is making. When it appears that the family is coping successfully with their crisis, the caseworker withdraws (Frazer 1978).

In some instances, when a history of child abuse, an uncooperative attitude, and severe and obviously inflicted injuries exists, *involuntary intervention* occurs. Usually this type of treatment plan is investigated and monitored by a "family court," a "juvenile court," a "children's court," or another court by a similar name. However, this type of plan can be used only if the child's injuries are clearly categorized under the state law.

To initiate a court proceeding, an investigator must file a *petition* with the court. A petition states that the court has jurisdiction in the matter and lists the *allegations* or charges of abuse. The *petitioner* is the person or agency that files the petition in the court. In most cases the agency is the Department of Social Services (Frazer 1978).

If the court accepts the petition, it assumes jurisdiction over the case. Then the court holds at least four hearings. The first is called the *advisement*. The *respondents*, usually the parents, are formally notified of the allegations of the petition and their rights in the proceedings. In most states the parents are entitled to a trial by jury. In all states the parents are entitled to retain their own attorney.

The second hearing is called the *setting*. This is the time when all parties can agree together on a time to resolve the allegations. The third hearing is called the *adjudicatory hearing*. At this hearing the basic question is settled: has the child been abused? If the child's injuries do not fit under the state law, and the parents' behavior cannot be classified as child abuse under the law, all legal proceedings cease. However, if it is judged a case of child abuse, one more hearing, called the *disposition*, occurs. At this hearing the treatment plan is decided on, and the custody of the child is determined.

The treatment program for the family is limited by the services available in the community. In rural areas treatment might include some or all of these services: Parents Anonymous, group counseling, psychiatry, individual counseling, homemaker services, parent aides or lay counselors, a therapeutic play school, and a residential treatment home.

In solving the problem of who has custody of the child, the court can do any of the following (Frazer 1978):

▪ Leave the child with his parents and provide treatment, monitoring the family until it shows it is coping successfully with its problems.

▪ Place the child in foster care, provide treatment, and monitor the family until it appears it is coping successfully enough with its problems that it is safe to return the child.

▪ Take the child out of the home permanently and set up the process for adoption proceedings to take place. (This is not an option in some states.)

More options are becoming available as more research and data is being collected on what alternatives serve the "best interests of the child." Some of these options will be discussed in a later chapter.

One statement must be made: about 10 percent of the total group of abusing parents are very seriously ill—too ill to benefit from any type of treatment. For these parents only one option is possible—to end the caregiving relationship. This may be done by placing the child with relatives or in permanent foster care or by formally terminating parental rights, to be followed by adoption (Kempe, R. and Kempe, C. H. 1978).

The remaining 90 percent of abusing parents have the potential to be helped. These parents are very sensitive to rejection and desperately need a long-term relationship with a friendly adult. Successful treatment programs use this premise as a starting point, whether the treatments take place in a home setting or a residential treatment center. However, the key is that if the family actively seeks help, the treatment is much more likely to be successful.

You Can Campaign for Children's Rights

Most people would agree that children are entitled to a safe home environment where they can grow and develop to their fullest potential and their greatest capability. The difficult question to answer in our democratic society is this: at what precise point should the state intervene when parents are not providing a safe environment for their children? On one hand, the parents have a "right" to raise their child as they see fit, but on the other hand, the child has a "right" to receive reasonable care and protection and to be free of cruel and inhuman punishment.

Traditionally, children have been entitled to custody, not rights. They have been entitled to legal protection through child labor laws and child maltreatment laws. They have not legally been entitled to decide where or with whom they will live, whether or not they will go to school, whether or not they can work, and where they can work.

However, some states have statutes that assume children have rights. For example, when a child is old enough to bear children, they have legal rights and responsibilities over that child. Because teen-aged parenting is occurring more often, courts, parents, grandparents, and the media are paying more attention to these legal rights.

Sources of Children's Rights

Child protection rights may evolve from several different sources: constitutional decisions, statutory law, and expansion of sources such as malpractice law.

Children's rights based on the U.S. *Constitution* evolve from decisions made by the U.S. Supreme Court as it interprets the U.S. Constitution. Only a decade ago the U.S. Supreme Court ruled that children had constitutional rights. The case was Tinker versus Des Moines Independent School District—the right of free speech as it applied to the right to wear antiwar armbands in school (Rose 1979).

Since then, other rights that apply to children have been determined by the Supreme Court. These rights include the following:

- Freedom from racial discrimination.
- Some freedom of speech—limited by the school's need for discipline.
- Some procedural rights—in dealing with school suspension.
- Some right to privacy—an individual's right to determine physical and mental processes.

Children's rights based on *statutes* have evolved from the statutory laws made by state legislatures or Congress. These laws have expanded children's rights beyond those named in the Constitution. For example, no Constitutional right exists for a child to be free from abuse and neglect. However, the law requiring reporting of child abuse and neglect implies that each child has the right to be free of that threat to life and health. All states and territories now have protective statutes and laws that assume basic child protective rights.

The final source of expanded children's rights is the *malpractice law*. As standards for the profession of child care are raised and clarified, a greater number of cases will be brought on behalf of children who have suffered because the basic standards have not adequately been met. As a greater number of mothers of young children move into the work force, demands for quality day care will increase. This demand will pressure states to establish more stringent standards and practices for day care, and an increasing number of cases will be initiated.

One Way to Insure Children's Rights

One radical but probably very effective way to improve children's safety and insure their well-being would be to make them full citizens, entitled to all rights except voting. This would mean that parents could not refuse their children basic health services. A baby's weight gain, immunization series, checks for birth defects, and child guidance could be left to parents' discretion, or they could be monitored by health professionals, as is true in many families right now. However, for this type of monitoring system to work effectively, society would have to agree that it was for the best interests of the family, not "for" the child and "against" the family. If health workers, doctors, and social service providers could intervene early, families seeking help and treatment could receive them before the child is hurt or damaged.

Just as everyone is an observer, also everyone must be a concerned advocate for children's rights. As child abuse and neglect workers join hands to exchange information and to discuss programs and treatment, they must also increase their lobbying for further recognition of children's rights.

The U.N. Declaration of the Rights of the Child

In November 1959 the United Nations declared ten basic rights for every child in the world. Although many countries, including our own, do not insure these basic rights for children, they serve as a reminder, or guide, for legal decisions, educational programs, and our own thinking. We list here those ten basic rights.

- The right to affection, love, and understanding.
- The right to adequate nutrition and medical care.
- The right to free education.
- The right to full opportunity for play and recreation.
- The right to a name and nationality.
- The right to special care, if handicapped.
- The right to be among the first to receive relief in times of disaster.
- The right to learn to be a useful member of society and to develop individual abilities.
- The right to be brought up in a spirit of peace and universal brotherhood.
- The right to enjoy these rights, regardless of race, color, sex, religion, national, or social origin.

To champion these basic rights is to realize that
ultimately our children's future and our world's future are
one and the same.

You Can Become a Child and Family Advocate

Webster defines *advocacy* as the act of speaking or
writing in support of something or someone. An advocate for
the child and the family tends to speak or write in favor of
the protection of children's rights and needs and the optimal
development of families. Besides speaking and writing, an
advocate must *act* in order to be effective. Many
opportunities and activities are valuable and worthwhile to
the cause.

Sometimes the most effective action starts at home. If you
know an isolated or lonely parent in your neighborhood or
community, reach out and befriend that person. Young
mothers are often so tied down to their homes by their
children that they need an occasional relief or a break from
the routine. Neighbors and friends can start a baby-sitting
group, a cooperative, a parent-relief club, or even a foster
grandparent service. Sometimes the most effective programs
start small and touch only a few people but serve as excellent
models to others wanting to see how successful programs are
accomplished.

Another goal to consider as a family advocate is to find
out what agencies and organizations are working on the
preventive aspects of child abuse and neglect. Volunteer your
services and talents. Any organization always has need for
volunteer services.

If you belong to a service group, a church group, or a
fraternal organization, request that child abuse and neglect
be added as a topic on the program schedule. Qualified
speakers are in every community, but if you can't obtain one,
you can study the problem and present the program.

Another project always needed is the *coordination* of services to the abused child and his family. If a lack of these services exists, begin planning to organize some. Find out what is being done and what needs to be done, and try to fill these gaps. Educate yourself about the child-abuse and neglect laws in your state so that you have the correct information about protective agencies and prevention programs.

With the help of others, you can encourage the establishment of a crisis hotline or a warm "tot line" for families who are in trouble or who need information about the progress of their child's growth and development.

Perhaps you live in a rural area where day-care services are lacking, either for full-time care or occasional drop-in care. Organize a meeting to talk about the problem. Bring together community leaders and explain what is needed to provide day care for children and parents.

Approach your school system and inquire about the educational programs that help prevent abuse and neglect. If they do not have any programs in child development, parenting, or family-living skills, volunteer to organize a group of parents to help write goals, objectives, and curricula for such classes.

Try to promote the development of good service-delivery programs to high-risk families. Work with existing agencies such as the local protective service department and private agencies. Support effective agencies that deliver direct treatment programs to families needing help in solving crises involving abuse and neglect.

Sometimes only one person is needed to get an organizational job done, but usually "model" programs are the result of many people working together in cooperation and dedication toward specific goals and objectives. Community efforts, like individual and group actions, can work toward child abuse prevention in many ways:

- Call together a group of representative community leaders involved in the child abuse problem and choose a leader.
- Pull together information on available resources in the area.
- Contact state and other governmental offices concerned with the problem.
- Organize a working team. Define goals and objectives and outline specific steps to achieve them.
- Print a resource book; establish a registry or a bank of information.
- Hold a training meeting.
- Call a public awareness meeting.
- Constantly evaluate progress. Change your direction or adjust your strategy if necessary.

Prevention is the only key that will solve the child-abuse and neglect problem. If concerned citizens focus their attention on prevention, others will join in to help.

Any advocacy movement will be accompanied by conflict. This is especially true in advocacy for children who have no literal or figurative voice of their own. However, with the divorce rate increasing, well over one million children a year go through custody hearings and procedures. More than two million children are currently excluded from school for various reasons, such as truancy or lack of toilet training. Hundreds of thousands of children are in institutions (Drotman and Goldstein 1977).

Clearly, no one speaks for these children. Most often they have life-altering decisions made for them by persons with no personal interest in them (the court, the school, or an institution). If you don't speak for these children, they may not get the rights coming to them. Individuals can become involved in combating this serious and growing problem. Ask yourself how you can be a part of preventing child abuse and neglect through advocacy.

5
Bright Spots
in the Child-Abuse
and Neglect Problem

At times the problem of child abuse and neglect seems overwhelmingly distressing: yet some bright spots have occurred in the last decade. Although we still have many miles to travel before we reach the end of the road, we now know more about how to get around some of the barriers blocking our path.

Growing Public Awareness

One of the biggest barriers to solving the problem of child abuse and neglect has been the silence, the secrecy and mystery surrounding it. Because of a growing number of educational programs and projects, increased media

117

coverage, and written materials, the general public is slowly becoming aware of the nature of child abuse and neglect.

The realization that everyone has a responsibility in the management of the program is the next step after awareness. These steps have been accomplished in many ways. Let us look at some of them.

Speakers' Bureaus

Over the last few years many professional groups have been established in large cities for the sole purpose of helping people become aware of the dynamics of child abuse and neglect. Awareness has to be ongoing to be effective. It has to emanate from many settings to reach the entire populace. Most speakers' bureaus have begun with a few knowledgeable professionals who actively participate with children and families in crisis. Because these professionals are usually so personally touched by their work, they tend to talk about it to others. They are asked to speak to groups, and soon the offers to speak are more numerous than they can handle. They realize that cooperation from others is essential to getting the job done; so they form a speakers' bureau involving a variety of professionals.

If you want a speaker to present a program on the incidence of child abuse and neglect in your area, you might contact one or more of the following resources:
Child Protective Service Unit
Crisis Hotline
Crisis Nursery
Community College—Child-Development Department
Hospital—Pediatrics Department
Parents Anonymous
Pediatrician
Police Department—Child-Abuse Detail
Public Library
School District—Child-Abuse and Neglect Liaison

Sheriff Department—Child-Abuse Detail
University—Child-Development Department

If these organizations do not operate a speakers' bureau themselves, they will direct you to others who can provide you speakers, audio-visual materials, and information.

Public Library Involvement

Another force for public awareness is the involvement of local libraries. Often they focus on societal problems by highlighting newly acquired written material and inviting speakers to discuss the topic. Many times high school and community-college libraries become centers for books, films, filmstrips, slides, and tapes concerning child abuse and neglect. These are public facilities frequented by a variety of people of all age groups. They are able to present sensitive material in a nonthreatening way.

Professional Updating

More and more preservice and inservice training in various helping professions include material on child abuse and neglect. Because identification and prevention is most effective with early observation, professionals who have contact with parents can become an informational source. These professionals include physicians, nurses, day-care workers, clergy, educators, social workers, law-enforcement officers, legal workers, and many others. At annual conferences and regularly scheduled training meetings, child abuse and neglect is appearing more and more as a topic for speakers and discussants.

Usually the type of child-abuse information presented falls into these categories:

- The dynamics, characteristics, and proportions of existence of child abuse and neglect.
- The management of stress and crisis.
- The type of therapeutic and rehabilitative services available.

Professionals as well as lay persons also need to know that prevention and treatment begin before the child is born; that families can be helped; that everyone is a valuable resource to the family and community to assist in that help; and that anyone can become a contributing and working team member (Kinsworthy 1978).

If professionals do not have a background in this subject, they need specific training coupled with follow-up training, then provision for ongoing training. This training is being done in many cities in the United States, and it is usually successful because professionals can in turn increase their colleagues' knowledge and their community's understanding by sharing what they have learned.

Colleges and universities can be tapped as a resource for consultation and current research to aid in the development of professional training programs on child abuse and neglect. Sometimes schools of higher education are funded to provide this type of community outreach. They may have organized speakers' bureaus or training programs available for the asking.

Increased professional awareness also aids in the prevention process. Primary prevention focuses on preventing the first occurrence of child abuse or neglect in a family. In order for this type of prevention to be effective, it has to be coordinated so that a crisis can be prevented. Although it is a way to reach out to families in need of help, it cannot be seen as an accusing action. Professionals who have a thorough understanding of the nature of the problem can provide this coordinated prevention method in a nonthreatening manner.

In many states, prevention has not been high on the priority list. More often emergency measures and after-the-fact treatment, because of the crisis nature, have been given greater attention. However, increased public awareness can help balance the scale. Certainly treatment for both the child and his family is important, and resources must go toward these aspects of the problem, but primary prevention can also be a long-term solution to the problem. The child-abuse and neglect programs that achieve this balance have strong public-awareness components.

The National Center on Child Abuse and Neglect

The agency having the greatest effect on public awareness is probably the National Center on Child Abuse and Neglect. In 1974 the President signed into law legislation that mandated the creation of this center. Placed under the wing of the Health, Education, and Welfare's Children's Bureau, the center has conducted studies and made grants to states and to public and private social-service agencies studying and working on the child abuse problem.

Posters such as those on the following page have helped get the message out to the public.

The Volunteer's Role

The role of the volunteer in increased public awareness has been the single most effective factor in raising public consciousness. Volunteers have provided public education through talks at conferences and service clubs, through media spots and films, and through distribution of publications. They have lobbied for better child protection legislation, testified at hearings, and advocated proposed legislation.

Some of these volunteer groups are senior citizens, some are professionals, and some are composed entirely of young mothers. One thirty-member all-volunteer group organized and held four large educational meetings in as many years. These meetings were open to anyone in the country. In conjunction with these conferences, they developed their own radio spots and wrote and printed accompanying brochures. They constructed a prevention kit that was given to all new mothers at hospitals, placed in doctors' offices and hospital waiting rooms, and distributed at childbirth education meetings. These volunteers also handled hundreds

Being a parent is one of the toughest jobs in the world.

Everyday pressures can become unbearable.
Sometimes you may strike out at someone you love—
your child, perhaps. We're here to help.

For more information write to the
NATIONAL CENTER ON CHILD ABUSE AND NEGLECT
U.S. CHILDREN'S BUREAU
P.O. Box 1182, Washington, D.C. 20013

2000 children will die this year from child abuse and neglect.

That's more than typhoid fever,
diphtheria, scarlet fever, polio,
and smallpox combined. There
is no vaccine. Only you can help.

For more information write to the
NATIONAL CENTER ON
CHILD ABUSE AND NEGLECT
U.S. CHILDREN'S BUREAU
P.O. Box 1182, Washington, D.C. 20013

There are two victims of child abuse and neglect.

1. The child.
2. The parent.
Both need help.

For more information write to the
NATIONAL CENTER ON
CHILD ABUSE AND NEGLECT
U.S. CHILDREN'S BUREAU
P.O. Box 1182, Washington, D.C. 20013

of speaking engagements, including PTA groups and teacher inservice meetings. As a result of the committee's efforts, a multidisciplinary organization was established to take over some of the responsibilities the committee could no longer handle. Because of the activities of these volunteers toward increased public awareness, reports of incidents of child abuse and neglect increased more than five-fold in their area (Northern Virginia Mental Health Association 1974).

The involvement of professionals on a volunteer basis has been essential in many child-abuse and neglect programs. In fact, concerned professionals are often the catalyst in the original formation of child-abuse and neglect projects. They may take the role of consultant, providing training for lay persons, or they may become involved in the coordination of services and agencies. In some lay-person organizations, professional volunteers are not only used as organizers but also as advisers and sponsors.

Social workers, physicians, psychologists, nurses, ministers, and other professionals can and do act as volunteer resource people. They have knowledge of other resources in the community of which the lay person may not be aware.

Nurse volunteers play an important role in crisis nurseries or centers. These volunteers have a direct service capacity that often is invaluable to the ongoing survival of such a center. When nurse volunteers take on the supervisory role, other nonprofessional volunteers can work alongside in order to expand the services.

Physicians who volunteer their services are important assets to any program. They can identify and enlist other resources in the area, both human and technical. But most important, they add credibility and status to a program. The authority of a physician can be valuable in raising public awareness and in lobbying and testifying at legislative hearings.

One does not have to be a professional to become a child advocate and to raise public awareness. Children do not have an official spokesperson. Child advocates can be their voice in meetings where decisions are being made that affect the future health and well-being of children. They can defend children when children's opinions and ideas are discounted as having no worth. A child advocate is constantly putting himself in the child's shoes, trying to see the world from the child's point of view. Professionals and lay persons can be effective child advocates. They may or may not have children of their own; they might not even work with children. The only requirement for a child advocate is that he be willing to respond to the child's needs and be sensitive to insure that the child's best interests are served.

Currently, both professional and lay volunteers are the core of many child-abuse and neglect programs across the country. The extent to which they are used depends on the type of program and its needs. No doubt volunteers play a unique role and offer a valuable contribution to child-abuse and neglect problems. When they are involved in such an important cause, they tend to discuss it with family, friends, relatives, neighbors, and colleagues; so the public becomes aware of the problem and also how the problem is being treated in their community. Volunteers demonstrate how public awareness works at its best.

If Abusive Parents Seek Help, Success Rate Is High

Another bright spot in the shadows of child abuse and neglect is that if abusive parents reach out and seek help for their problem, the success rate for effective solution is high. Parents who see themselves as needing professional help and treatment have taken the first step. This may be the most important step they will take toward being healed.

Unfortunately, a shadow on this bright spot is that most parents do not see themselves as needing help. When they are approached by a professional investigating their case, many resist the help or treatment that is offered. Many, if not most, abusive parents do not recognize their problem behavior unless it is pointed out to them. However, most can be helped if the seriousness of the problem hits them with impact. Many abusive parents can be helped if they are identified soon enough and want to change their ways.

The availability of nonthreatening resources, such as anonymous telephone-help lines or call-in programs often allows parents seeking help to initiate that first step more readily.

How Do Abusive Parents Know If They Need Help?

If you are a parent reading this book, you may see yourself in some of the categories that define abusive behavior. Perhaps you are wondering just what to do about it. Self-identification is important in solving the problem, and you may be ready to take some important steps.

First, ask yourself some question: "Is my life totally out of control?" "Am I in crisis right at this moment?" "Am I flirting with a potentially dangerous situation?" Perhaps you have a relationship with your children that has not yet developed into a crisis situation but you fear that it might. Either way, you need to take some immediate action.

To help you identify the specific problem, answer further questions as honestly as you can:

- Do I feel as if my life is out of control?
- Do I behave in ways that are out of control?
- Do I feel I am a very poor parent?
- Do I hate myself for some of the things I do to my child?
- Do I hurt my child because I am angry with myself?
- Do I hurt my child because I am frustrated with someone else?
- Was I abused as a child?
- Am I suspicious and distrustful of other people?
- Do I feel lonely and alienated from those around me?
- After really punishing my child severely, do I feel disgusted with myself or ashamed?

- Have I ever injured my child, then lied about it, saying such things as "He ran into the door," "He fell out of bed," "He tumbled down the stairs," or "He fell off his bike?"
- Do I make elaborate vows never again to behave in certain ways—and then do the very thing I made a vow not to do?
- Do I want help?

If you answer "yes" more than "no" to these questions, you may want to seek help as soon as possible. Remember, you are not alone. Many parents feel as you do, have reached out for help, and have solved their problem.

What Steps Can Abusive Parents Take To Get Help?

The first step is very important: *Reach out for help.* If you have identified the problem and want to get help, you can do it. Almost every community has at least one of the following helping organizations or agencies.

Check your phone book for these listings:

- Child Protective Services: Most agencies have counselors available twenty-four hours a day to talk with parents.
- Crisis nurseries (or daycare centers): Most nurseries have facilities to take children, day or night, when they become too much to handle. Sometimes the best immediate solution is to put your child in another environment temporarily. A day or two with your child out of the house may help you seek additional aid.
- Police or sheriff's department: Many departments have specifically trained personnel for counseling, intervening, or helping in crisis situations.
- Parents Anonymous: Most PA groups meet weekly or twice a week to share common problems of abuse and neglect.
- Family counseling centers: These organizations may be public or private in nature, but many can provide emergency services as well as long-term counseling.

■ Churches: There are concerned, caring clergy in every community who can respond effectively in crisis situations as well as provide ongoing support for families.

If you are near the end of your rope, don't do anything drastic; help is available. Try a phone call to any of these groups, organizations, or agencies. They have been successful in helping many families get their feet back on the ground. They have skills and abilities to help you solve your problem.

After you have taken the first step—reaching out for immediate help—a second step is to *work with a person or group of people who can give you support and counseling over a period of time.* Your problem didn't occur overnight, and you can't expect it to disappear quickly.

Parents Anonymous groups have been very effective in providing self-help therapy for abusive and neglecting individuals. Families have been helped by counselors and therapists who treat each member individually as well as together. These two support methods as well as others can be obtained from organizations and agencies previously listed.

A third important step toward solving your problem is to *invest in some good parenthood education.* Fortunately, this type of education comes in many different topics, delivery media, and timelines.

Here are some of the topics you may to focus on:
■ discipline
■ communication
■ problem-solving
■ child rearing
■ relationships
■ roles
■ developmental levels
■ decision-making
■ other related topics

And information about these topics can be found in the following delivery media:

- courses
- classes
- conferences
- seminars
- discussion groups
- television programs
- radio programs
- newspaper articles
- magazine articles
- books
- pamphlets
- movies
- slide series
- film strips
- other related media

These delivery media may have the following timelines and places:

- a yearly course at a university
- a semester course at a community college
- a short course at a school, church, or agency
- a weekly meeting in your community
- a day-long conference or seminar
- an hour-long program on TV or radio
- many other combinations.

Remember, those authorities who have worked with abusive and neglectful individuals say that if abusive parents seek help for their problem, the success rate is high for effective solution. Reach out and take that first step.

Research into Causes, Prevention, and Remediation

Another bright spot has been the increasing amount of research coming out of abuse-project centers, colleges and universities, and hospitals. In the last decade child abuse and neglect have been topics of many research papers and theses. Most of this child-abuse research has been focused on identification of the causes of child maltreatment. Three different approaches have been tried. One approach has been to study the mental health of the abusive parent. Many studies have examined the parent's attitudes and beliefs after the abuse has occurred. Another approach has been to examine how society figures in the picture and the role the environment takes in causing child abuse and neglect. A third type of research has looked at the victim and has attempted to analyze the role the child plays in causing the abuse.

Although each type of research has approached the subject from a different angle and each method has been different, no single model sufficiently explains causes of abuse. Consequently, no treatment based exclusively on any one approach can expect to eliminate or significantly reduce child abuse.

The conclusion many authorities have reached is that the psychiatric state of the abusing parent, the stresses of the family's environment, and the characteristics of the child are all intertwined and interrelated. Child abuse and neglect cannot be examined piece-by-piece but only as a whole; therefore, a few current maltreatment studies have focused on the whole family and its environment. Although studies are increasing, many questions are still unanswered. Each new piece of research may answer another part of the puzzle, but it also raises new questions that will have to be dealt with in the future.

Concept of Keeping Biological Family Together

Another bright spot in the child-abuse and neglect problem is the concept that children are better off with their natural or biological families than with foster families or in institutions. This is true, of course, unless physical or mental harm is dealt the child, threatening his health and well-being. Simply removing children from abusing and troubled parents will not solve the problem of child abuse. Nor will it prevent child abuse from occurring in the future. In fact, placing an abused child in an institution is often another form of abuse. Specifically, this placement encourages further abuse and neglect by a society and a bureaucracy pretending to protect the child. Foster-care institutionalization sometimes becomes a temporary dumping ground for children because treatment, support systems, and services are not available. The problem is complicated by the slow process of court systems and agencies. Some children are left in limbo for extended periods of time, even up to three to five years—years that may be the most formative of their lives. The younger the child, the more important it is that he have a continuing, nurturing relationship.

According to research and experience, most child-abuse authorities agree that the best approach is to keep families together whenever possible. At the same time, every attempt should be made to correct the parental misbehavior through treatment programs and thus prevent the abuse from recurring.

Money spent on prevention and treatment programs is not only humanitarian, it is cost-effective; it is the only way to break the cycle of violence from generation to generation.

The programs that are focused on helping and treating the whole family are more successful in the short run. However, the big difference will probably be seen over several generations. Breaking the cycle of violence is not a quick and easy task, but it can be done. Keeping families together seems to be one positive step toward that goal.

Helping Families by Friendshipping

Reports from many communities suggest that another bright spot in the rehabilitation of abusive parents is the nonprofessional worker who spends considerable time with the family. This person has many different names: lay therapist, parent aide, volunteer aide, surrogate family aide, or just "visiting friend"—a term describing the role accurately and inoffensively. The focus and orientation of these programs may differ, but they all have one common factor: the visitor to the family spends enough time to develop a meaningful friendship with the family. Because of the time involved, these visitors may work with only two or three families at a time. A caseload of this size allows the visitor to provide what trained social workers and professional counselors do not have the time to give—warm, loving support and "mothering" or "nurturing" care. Specifically, the visitor is a close friend who can give the emotional backup required when a family suffers through a crisis.

According to some authorities, parents who abuse their children did not receive adequate love and nurturing as children (Barry 1976). Many studies, as we have said, suggest that abusive parents were usually abused themselves.

Other studies suggest that most abusive parents didn't learn to trust others when they were children. This inability to trust makes it difficult to develop even casual relationships later in life. When these parents expect and demand nurturing love from their children—the love that no one else has ever given them—they set up an abusive situation. Because children are incapable of providing nurturing love, they are punished.

Communities report that the success of "visiting friends" suggests that a warm, nurturing person can break this cycle. By meeting some of the parents' emotional needs later on in life and by physically, emotionally, and socially demonstrating what real friendship is all about, they can alter the abusive cycle.

Abusive parents reach an important milestone when they trust the visitor enough to call for help when they are unable to cope. The call usually takes the place of lashing out at the child or taking some other violent action. Abusive parents may even go through a childlike phase as they experience,

maybe for the first time, the emotional support that most
people receive as children. After the initial experience they
gradually outgrow this dependency and become stronger on
their own. The visiting aide then becomes a backup for
unusually stressful situations.

How long and to what extent the visiting friend works
with the family depends on the type of program and the
needs of the family. The duration and intensity vary among
programs and between families. Some visiting friends might
make daily visits at the beginning, and others might visit only
two or three times a week. However, the visiting friend must
be available twenty-four hours a day and on weekends since
crisis situations often do not occur during usual working
hours. Some programs provide backup aides to cover for the
visiting friends when they are unavailable.

Involvement with a family varies greatly, also. A "visiting
friend" may work with a family only six months or up to two
years. However, visits usually taper off after the first few
months. Because real bonds of friendship develop, a complete
cutoff may never occur. The occasional call reporting that
the family has stabilized and is doing well is a positive
reward for the visiting friend. It also provides the visiting
friend great encouragement to keep on working with current
families in crisis.

The key element that seems to make the lay-person or
paraprofessional programs work is the fact that abusive
parents rarely see the "visiting friend" as a threat. Social
workers and other professionals often find their authority and
the bureaucracies they represent to be barriers between
clients and themselves. The paraprofessional aides often serve
as a liaison between abusive parents and professionals; they
can act as advocates for the family, pointing out needs that
no one else perceives.

Most programs claim that child battering rarely recurs in
homes where "visiting friends" have worked intensively.
However, isolating the actual impact of these

paraprofessional programs is difficult because often other treatment programs are occurring simultaneously. Although precise statistical data may be difficult to pin down, "visiting friends" provide what may be the only practical way to allow one person to focus attention on families who need strong emotional backup and support (Barry 1976).

The Team Approach

Another bright spot in the child-abuse and neglect problem is that teams of professionals and paraprofessionals are working together to provide prevention, direct services, and treatment for the family in crisis. Schools, hospitals, agencies, probation departments, self-help groups, parent groups, and courts are cooperating in joint efforts to help the child and his family. The team approach seems to work most effectively when the role of each of these service-providers is clearly defined.

Two ingredients are necessary to providing a successful community-wide program. First, a local body or agency must assume ultimate responsibility for implementing the coordination and monitoring the service plan involving all team members. This type of leadership helps to define each team member's role. It also helps to eliminate duplication of services, rendering the whole operation more cost-effective. The coordinating authority may vary from state to state, from community to community, and from program to program. In some places a private child-welfare agency may do the job; in other areas the state agency, the mental health center, or the school administration may provide coordination. When the coordinator is chosen rather than mandated, the success rate appears to be considerably higher.

A second important ingredient to the team approach is an intensive public-information campaign. Programs using the team approach report that no matter how tightly it is structured or how smoothly it is coordinated, it is ineffective if no one uses it or if citizens do not have confidence in it.

If a teacher does not know whom to turn to if a sick or injured child appears in the classroom; if a concerned relative has no idea where to call about an abused niece, nephew, or grandchild; if a neighbor doesn't know what to do about an infant's screams at three o'clock in the morning, the coordinated team approach is not working. Team members must get the message out to the public. Attempting coordination of team members and launching a public information campaign is a big job, but in many communities it has been accomplished with effective results.

The makeup of the teams are as diverse as the areas they serve. Since each state and community has different needs, the composition of the teams varies with the programs, the services available, and the structure of service-providers.

A MultiDisciplinary Consultation Team

One of the more common groupings in large cities is called a multidisciplinary consultation team. This team may consist of a social worker, a psychiatrist, a nurse, an attorney, a police officer, a pediatrician, and a school liaison officer. The team leader might be the child's protective-service case worker who is assigned to the case. The professionals would be available for consultation, advice, and decision-making at the case worker's request (Steiner 1978).

The multidisciplinary consultation team can also play a major role in the early detection of high-risk families in the precrisis stage. It can provide consulting services to the team leader to determine an appropriate, individualized treatment plan. It can also help determine whether to remove a child from his home, or if he has been previously removed, whether to return him.

One of the most useful and natural functions of this team is to point out inadequacies and fragmentations of services in the community. Also, team members can facilitate community-wide communication, so important to the success of the multidisciplinary approach.

The Hospital-Based Diagnostic Team

Another team approach is the hospital-based diagnostic team. Its members include a pediatrician, a psychologist, and a hospital social worker. These people are specially trained to diagnose and treat the medical, psychological, and psychiatric aspects of child abuse and neglect. The team is also responsible for reporting suspected cases of child abuse and neglect to the child protective service worker and providing assistance in identification of questionable cases.

The team has several purposes: it provides consultation for physicians or other professionals who are not specially trained in child abuse and neglect; it supports the child protective worker in assessing cases and developing treatment plans; it facilitates help to children and families; it provides periodic inservice training for all emergency room personnel; and it may take the leadership in establishing a written hospital policy for suspected child abuse and neglect cases (Steiner 1978).

The School-Based Diagnostic Team

The school-based diagnostic team consists of the principal or the school liaison, the school nurse, and the school psychologist or a representative from the counseling and guidance department. The identified child's teacher is also part of the team. Usually the principal coordinates the team activities, but not always.

The purpose of the team varies from state to state and from district to district. Depending on the size of the school district and its personnel, the team might accomplish any or all of the following (Steiner 1978):

■ Establish a written school policy on child abuse and neglect.

- Pinpoint suspected cases and help identify high risk families for preventive interaction.
- Report suspected child abuse and neglect.
- Develop a child protective service feedback system.
- Promote a community-awareness system.
- Promote and conduct inservice education and team training.
- Establish an on-going evaluation of the program itself.

The school team keeps careful records, especially records on reported incidents. They take care to keep confidential both the reports and those whom the reports concern. Although the team approach is a good way to broaden the visibility of child abuse and neglect, anyone else working with the child has both the right and the responsibility to report suspected cases of child abuse and neglect.

The Crisis Intervention Team

The crisis intervention team, or mobile diversion specialists, as they are sometimes called, are highly skilled interveners who go into homes during crisis situations. They respond to a variety of psychological, sociological, economic, and family problems. They provide counseling to resolve immediate problems and facilitate referral to appropriate social-service agencies for further assistance. Usually they initiate short-term follow-up to insure that the resolution of the crisis or referral to the agency has been successful.

The team may be based at a police station, but team members are usually civilian. They are on call twenty-four hours a day, seven days a week. The team can save many hours of time for law-enforcement officers. For example, they can help reduce repeated offenses; they can act as a liaison between the public and the law-enforcement professionals; and they can have a big part in the improvement of community relations.

One of the primary functions of this team is to be an advocate for children and juveniles. Whenever possible, they divert juveniles and other "noncriminals" from the criminal justice system.

In rural areas, the team may work out of the county sheriff's office, and the "team" may be only one person; but the job can still be accomplished (Steiner 1978).

The team approach may be more difficult to organize and structure, but after it begins operating, it usually is far more effective than agencies working independently. Sometimes one agency or another feels that it should carry through the entire process necessary for the protection of a child and his family; however, no one agency has all the resources necessary to determine what exactly has happened and how to best serve the family.

Also, occasionally philosophical conflicts occur among agencies sharing the responsibility for the management of child-abuse and neglect incidents. Agencies often have difficulty balancing their roles and developing teamwork when survival of the family and criminal prosecution are parts of the same case. However, this conflict points up a need for *greater* cooperation among agencies rather than *less*.

Because most child-abuse or neglect cases are not referred for criminal prosecution, law-enforcement officers have to seek solutions other than their usual ones. They have to become involved with a variety of community agencies. On the other hand, the officer might be the first agency personnel that a social-worker, a school-liaison person, or a physician might encounter in the case. These situations point to the efficiency and practicality of a team approach. Ultimately, teamwork is necessary for suspected child maltreatment to come to a reasonable and safe conclusion for the child and his family.

The cooperation necessary for teamwork among the service agencies does not arise out of an obligation toward another agency but toward the child and his family. The survival of the family unit must be uppermost in the mind of any professional working with child-abuse and neglect situations.

Community Therapeutic Services

Another bright spot in the child-abuse and neglect picture is the concept of community therapeutic services. These services provide an opportunity for the abused and neglected child to express his feelings, satisfy his emotional needs, and cope with a hostile home environment. These services vary among communities and usually are found in large cities rather than in rural areas. Community therapeutic services may include play groups, crisis nurseries, psychotherapy, and therapeutic day-care centers.

Play Groups

Play groups generally meet a few hours a week, often while parents are attending therapy sessions. These groups may have a professional staff, or they may be supervised by a professional but staffed by volunteer workers. While the children are playing together, their language, socialization, and behavior patterns can be observed and analyzed. Often, problems that have gone unnoticed are discovered. With the proper diagnosis, appropriate treatment programs can be started.

Crisis Nurseries

Crisis nurseries offer immediate and short-term relief to parents temporarily unable to care for their children. The crisis nursery is a twenty-four-hour shelter facility that allows the parent some time out from parenting responsibilities. Perhaps the parent needs some time and energy to seek out an alternative plan in a precrisis or a crisis situation. The length of stay for the child ranges from a few hours to several days or weeks. The staff tries to keep the adult-child ratio low so that an unusual amount of time and attention can be given to the child. Usually the staff is professional and specially trained. However, volunteer helpers are essential to provide the low child-adult ratio needed. Often, intensive preservice training programs are mandatory before volunteers can work in the nursery. A common community concern is that the crisis nursery might be abused as a baby-sitting service. However, communities report that this is not true. If appropriate guidelines are established and the purpose of the nursery is explained, the community does not tend to abuse this important special facility.

Psychotherapy

Although psychotherapy is not needed by every abused or neglected child, it is essential in some cases. If a young child has serious emotional problems and exhibits abnormal behavior, intensive therapy should be available to him.

Some programs offer play therapy for preschool as well as school-aged abused or neglected children. Play therapy allows children to "act out" traumatic experiences in the presence of a nonthreatening adult. A play therapy room looks very much like a well-equipped preschool or day-care center, with art materials; a dress-up area; a play-house corner; dolls of every sex, age, color, and size; stand-up balloon toys to hit; boxing gloves; trikes; bikes; and so on. The child is allowed to play with these toys in any way he desires and to move freely from area to area. He may elect not to do anything at all; he may instead sit and look at the toys. An adult may enter into play with the child or passively observe his actions, or do both. The adult may carry on a questioning conversation with the child during the play time. The idea is to help the child act out or talk out the fears, anxieties, or scared feelings under the surface. The playroom is a place where imagination and fantasy reign. The child is encouraged to use his imagination with the toys in role-play situations.

Some programs offer play therapy for preschool as well as school-aged abused or neglected children. Play therapy allows children to "act out" traumatic experiences in the presence of a nonthreatening adult. A play therapy room looks very much like a well-equipped preschool or day-care center, with art materials; a dress-up area; a play-house corner; dolls of every sex, age, color, and size; stand-up balloon toys to hit; boxing gloves; trikes; bikes; and so on. The child is allowed to play with these toys in any way he desires and to move freely from area to area. He may elect not to do anything at all; he may instead sit and look at the toys. An adult may enter into play with the child or passively observe his actions, or do both. The adult may carry on a questioning conversation with the child during the play time. The idea is to help the child act out or talk out the fears, anxieties, or scared feelings under the surface. The playroom is a place where imagination and fantasy reign. The child is encouraged to use his imagination with the toys in role-play situations.

Another benefit of play therapy is that the child has the complete attention of a caring adult. For some children it may be the first time they ever have had a relationship with an adult on a one-to-one basis without being threatened, harmed, or neglected. Play-therapy rooms are often an integral part of treatment centers for abusive parents. They can also be found in hospitals and clinics that have long-term treatment facilities for abused or neglected children.

Therapeutic Day-Care Centers

Therapeutic day-care centers serve as a refuge for abused and neglected children from a few hours to ten or twelve a day. These centers provide the opportunity for an adult to observe the child's interaction with other children over a period of time. They can also offer a long-term therapy program for the abused child and his family. Only a few therapeutic day-care centers exist across the country, but all of them have one belief in common: they consider child abuse to be "family abuse." They run treatment programs for parents and children together, in the same setting—in the day-care center itself.

The therapeutic day-care center is compatible with the theory that abused children should not be taken away from their families except in extreme cases. This theory is based on the premise that families can and will change if the resources are available to them. Parental involvement is necessary at the outset of the therapeutic day-care-center program. In fact, no child can be enrolled without the promised cooperation of his parents.

After abused children are identified by courts, health clinics, hospitals, and schools, the big job is to convince parents to become a part of the therapeutic day-care-center program. One way the operators of the school do this without arousing too many feelings of fear and guilt in the parents is by totally accepting that parents do get out of control at the same time that they really do want to be good parents. With this attitude, the staff have been able to enroll parents, provide parental therapy, and educate them about normal child-development patterns.

Reports from staff members of such centers indicate that these parents need to know it is normal to find coping with children difficult. They need to know how to avoid struggles and power plays with their children. They need to understand how infants and toddlers grow and develop. And they must understand what can be expected of a child at a certain growth stage and age level.

Some of these centers have bus transportation that brings the child and the parent into the center each day. Other programs have evening and weekend meetings with parents, and the children also attend.

A strong requirement for these centers is a low adult-child ratio. Besides play, nap, snacks, and lunch, adults give the one-to-one attention and nurturing these children so badly need. Ages may range from infancy to five years of age, but usually the ages fall into the 2½ to four-year-old range. This is the age when children exhibit behavior showing they may be slow to trust and quick to care for themselves. One child may refuse to talk, knowing that his parents have severely punished him for crying too much. Another child may fall off his chair backwards and simply pick himself up, repressing his urge to cry and be comforted. Some children come from homes that are absolute chaos. These children may request the same routine, the same books read, the same games played, and the same songs sung every day. They may love the feeling of safety that comes from repetition of each day's activities.

Three basic goals permeate therapeutic day-care centers. First, they want to provide unlimited opportunities for children to act out their subconscious urges in play. If they have experienced traumas in the few short years of their lives, their feelings may already have a hard cover. Very young children learn to submerge feelings and behaviors they have been punished for. So in the psychotherapy playroom these children are encouraged to act out fears, angers, and problems with their peers and with their parents.

A second goal of such a program is basic socialization skills. Abused and neglected children often have not had consistent care and training in the basics of getting along. Center staff members have often commented that children entering the therapeutic day-care center for the first time might withdraw completely, or they might take the place over; no middle ground seems to exist. The basics of asking for a drink or for help in putting something on, of self-feeding, or of toilet training may be more immediate goals than requiring a "please" or a "thank you" or turn-taking—all of which would be common goals in a regular day-care center.

A third goal in a therapeutic day-care center is to help the child build a positive self-image, or a good picture of himself. An abused or neglected child tends to think of himself as a problem, or the cause of the abuse. He believes he has done something wrong, causing Mom or Dad to punish him severely. He may have experienced emotional abuse by constantly being put down, called a no-good, or simply discounted as having any worth. At age two to four children are building their self-image. In fact, child-development specialists believe that the way a person sees himself in later life develops before the age of five. So if a young child feels guilty about causing abuse, if he is rejected by his parents, and if he has suffered emotional abuse, building his positive self-image may be quite a challenge for the staff of the therapeutic day-care center.

The importance of providing treatment for abused and neglected children while they are very young is obvious for many reasons. However, one of the most apparent is that if a child is overladen with stress and guilt, he has no energy left for learning. Often abused children are "unavailable to learning." They block out new stimuli and experiences. When this occurs within the first five to seven years of life, the child misses the basics required for all life skills.

Effective Programs

Finally, one of the brightest spots in the child-abuse and neglect picture is a number of innovative programs designed to combat child maltreatment. Most of these program models have emerged within the last decade. Many have had a tightly structured research component. Their studies show they have had success at stopping the recurrence of abuse while keeping families together. Although the programs are organized and structured differently, they all aim to bolster the self-esteem of both the abusing parent and the abused child. According to organizers, their programs can be implemented in any community.

Although it is difficult to present a tally of children saved, most of these programs can point to a number of parents and children who have salvaged their self-esteem and have escaped the syndrome of maltreatment. Authorities have stated that any type of intervention program that keeps children from being abused or removes the child from a life-threatening situation is successful. And probably any type of intervention program can be successful if its organizers realize that parents and children need someone they can talk with and can trust.

Centers for Abuse and Neglect

One of the most successful centers for abuse and neglect is New York's Foundling Hospital. Dr. Vincent Fontana, a long-time leader in the child maltreatment field, is the medical director of this special hospital. In his book, *Somewhere A Child Is Crying* (1973), he discusses the Foundling's "human network" of support that is at the core of its program. This human network includes a multidisciplinary team of professionals and paraprofessionals who care for and educate young, poor, mostly unwed mothers. They are housed in a variety of locations: a hospital residential setting in which the mothers live with their children over a four-month period, half-way houses, and sometimes the patients' homes with out-patient services. There is also an emergency twenty-four-hour hotline. The program provides individual and group therapy, parenting and consumer education, emotional supports, emergency assistance, and activities to bolster the parents' self-esteem.

Although the Foundling Hospital deals with a hard-core, under-privileged and depressed population, its operators can claim that 75 percent of families have stayed together without further incidence of abuse. Dr. Fontana's regret is that the number of families they can treat in the program is a drop in the bucket compared with the number of families that need help.

The National Center for the Prevention and Treatment of
Child Abuse and Neglect in Denver, Colorado, is another
pioneering area in the field of child maltreatment. Under the
leadership of an outstanding authority, Dr. C. Henry Kempe,
the center has pioneered a number of innovative child-abuse
and neglect projects and programs (Donovan 1978):

■ a therapeutic play school for abused children
■ an interdisciplinary team training program
■ a scholar's program providing six-month grants to lawyers,
pediatricians, nurses, educators, journalists, and
anthropologists for study of child abuse and neglect at the
center
■ a foster-care training program to improve foster-care
placement and to facilitate communication between foster
and natural parents
■ a sexual-abuse program with therapy groups for sexually
abused children and adolescents and their parents
■ a lay health-visitor program that sends paraprofessionals to
the home of each new mother shortly after hospital discharge
to inform families of available resources, to help with
transportation, and to provide emotional support.

The Child Sexual Abuse Treatment Program in Santa
Clara County, California, is a successful model program for
sexual abuse and misuse. Director of the center, Dr. Henry
Giarretto, says that the core of the program consists of
principles of good parenting—that they be neither permissive
nor cruelly punitive. The offense is certainly not condoned,
but the offender is not rejected, either. The idea is to work
together to overcome the problem. This center works closely
with the criminal justice system to try to avoid a potentially
destructive effect it could have on a family. The staff of the
center found out quickly that traditional therapy alone would
not solve the problem of incest. They tried various
approaches but found that clients really must feel the caring
response of an entire community in order to face their

families and communities during and after treatment
(Dorman 1979).

Because such factors as funding sources, sponsoring
agencies, and treatment philosophies influence the design
and objectives of each maltreatment program, the ways in
which they are implemented are very different. Some
programs are privately funded and treat certain clientele;
others are publicly funded and treat a broader clientele.

In 1974 the Minnesota state legislature mandated the
commissioner of corrections to establish a statewide program
for victims of sexual abuse. This situation is unique to
Minnesota. The Program for Victims of Sexual Assault has
coordinated services and training throughout the state, has
acted as a clearing house for local projects, and has served as
a resource center for human and technical resources. It has
recently prepared a manual regarding incest for distribution
to police, hospitals, and criminal justice personnel throughout
Minnesota. In addition, seventeen centers serving all victims
of sexual assault have been established statewide to provide
crisis intervention, referrals, and counseling (Dorman 1979).

Another unusual program found in Knoxville, Tennessee,
was called the Sexual Abuse Helpline. It was under the
direction of the Child and Family Service Department. The
helpline offered a twenty-four-hour phone access to a highly
trained sex-abuse counselor.

Callers first heard a two-minute teletaped message
explaining sexual abuse; then they were encouraged to stay
on the line if they wished to speak to a counselor. They gave
the caller the option of anonymity if he wished it. Callers
received information and support.

On the average, Helpline received 1,000 calls per month.
Approximately 100 of the callers would stay on the line past
the recorded message. Half the calls concerned sexual abuse,
and half were related to other sexual, individual, and family
problems.

Contrary to popular assumption, boys reported sexual abuse almost as frequently as girls, and less than one percent of the calls involved homosexual abuse. Boys were more likely than girls to develop a supportive relationship with a counselor, but they would not allow the relationship to be reported officially. Approximately ten cases per month involving female victims were reported to the Department of Human Services; only one male victim could be reported.

Assessment by the project's evaluators indicated that the major benefit of the Sexual Abuse Helpline was increased community awareness. After funding ended, only the teletaped message, referring callers to a project office for further information and aid, was maintained.

The Knoxville experience highlights the important issue in establishing a treatment program: community awareness may increase the reporting rate to such an extent that the project agencies become overloaded. However, after a need is demonstrated, funding is usually easier to find, as is local support for expanded programs (Dorman 1979).

Self-Help Programs

Parents Anonymous, a self-help program similar to Alcoholics Anonymous, provides support for a group of people with parenting problems. Parents involved in the program are probably the best indicators of its effectiveness: a national evaluation showed that after one month's participation or less, verbal abuse decreased and physical abuse rarely reappeared.

The chapter meetings are the focus of the Parents Anonymous program. They are safe places where parents can express their frustration and anger without fear of judgment or condemnation. The emotional support at chapter meetings gives abusive parents practical alternatives for their behavior. They are helped to believe that destructive impulses and behaviors can be redirected into loving, nurturing behavior with far better results. Again, one of its goals is to help parents begin to appreciate their own worth and the value of their experiences. Involvement in Parents Anonymous helps increase a parent's self-esteem and strengthens his ability to handle stress and to cope with crisis.

Each chapter has ten parents. The chairperson is usually chosen from the group. The function of the chairperson is to lead the group and provide support and nurturing to other parents. The sponsor, usually a mental-health professional or a similar professional, functions as a backup resource to the chairperson.

Parents contact Parents Anonymous through their own initiative or through referrals from an agency such as Child Protective Services. Self-referrals are facilitated through various forms of publicity, such as speaking engagements, public meetings, pamphlet and poster distribution, and radio and television announcements.

Since the nature of Parents Anonymous is nonjudgmental and is supportive of parents, community awareness must be done in a nonthreatening manner. Therefore, publicity does not depict child abusers as monsters or as psychotics with unsolvable problems. Parents come to the realization that they can find solutions to their own problems and learn to feel better about themselves in the process.

In many Parents Anonymous chapters, parents also discuss ways to improve their child's self-esteem. They learn to praise children for specific behaviors, such as cleaning a room, picking up toys, or drawing a picture. Parents try to let their children know they are meaningful people in the household, and they have worth. They try to tell their child that no matter what he has done, he never deserved the abuse he received.

Parents Anonymous has hundreds of chapters across the country, and it is growing. Its national headquarters are located at 2810 Artesia Blvd., Redondo Beach, California 90278. Parents Anonymous works for parents, but the real beneficiary is the child.

Emergency Shelter and Care

Emergency services take immediate action in crises involving children and their families. Since some situations require immediate removal of a child from his home, emergency services can be called on twenty-four hours a day. In some areas emergency neighborhood crisis centers provide many functions to the immediate community. Some centers provide a police team or crisis intervention team on or near the facility. Primary emphasis is placed on prevention and early identification of families in crisis.

An *emergency shelter* for families provides temporary shelter for families whose home situation is inadequate or for those who have no home or have had to leave on an emergency basis. The goal is to keep families together so that they can support each other and move toward stability and independence. The services of a family emergency shelter include room and board for a specified period of time (usually two weeks), assessment of the family's problems and needs, social-service assistance, relocation assistance, transportation services, family counseling services, and follow-through.

An *emergency caretaker* provides responsible adult supervision of children when parents are unable to supervise their children or when there is no adult in the household to supervise. This insures the child's stay in a safe, secure, and familiar environment. It is a short-term service, usually relieved by a homemaker, a neighbor, a relative, or a returning parent.

The *emergency homemaker* is specially trained and assigned on a short- or long-term basis to teach and provide homemaking skills to families. This includes house management and basics such as cooking, budgeting, and child care. The homemaker extends the services of the caretaker. This type of service allows the family to remain in their own home in time of crisis and allows time for long-range planning. Usually the caretakers and homemakers are

150

indigenous to the area so that they are more easily accepted by the family and are familiar with the neighborhood and community.

Emergency foster homes provide short-term care, usually a month, for children who cannot be maintained in their own homes for some reason. Ideally, the foster home is in the same community or neighborhood as the child's, requiring of the child less emotional and physical readjustment.

Emergency shelter for adolescents provides care for older youths with special problems. The adolescent who cannot be handled in his own home or in a foster home and who doesn't fit in a juvenile detention facility can find a temporary refuge until something more permanent can be arranged. The ideal shelter provides both short- and long-term placement so that the adolescent can receive counseling services, learning experiences, and basic life-sustaining skills. The shelter provides the adolescent with adult supervision that can help the youth over a time of crisis and get him on his feet again.

Volunteer Programs

Because of increasing public awareness about child abuse and neglect, the role of volunteers in child abuse and neglect programs is expanding.

One of the most traditional roles for volunteers is that of fund-raiser. This role is especially critical in programs that receive little or no federal or state support. For example, at Casa de los Ninos, a temporary care facility in Tucson, Arizona, volunteers convinced local businesses, churches, service clubs, and individuals to donate a house and $165,000 in materials, money, and labor. This program is still totally dependent on the community for its annual budget. Volunteers donate hours of time toward fund-raising activities and events to maintain the ongoing budget of this special center.

Other traditional roles for volunteers that require little or no special skills or education include chauffeuring, organizing and coordinating, public awareness, and soliciting other volunteers and professionals. However, more innovative roles have developed for volunteers in the past decade. Many of these jobs have emerged from federal and state programs concerned with the treatment of child abuse and neglect. Parents' aides, lay therapists, and surrogate parents—such as foster grandparents—are roles that volunteers have been taking in recent years. Well-trained, carefully selected volunteers can perform in a variety of direct service roles in the treatment of abusive families. Program organizers have found mature adults willing to offer their time and talents in every community.

Abusive families often are socially isolated and lack the supportive network of friends and family. They may have an overwhelming need for warmth and support from others but do not have the knowledge or skills to reach out for it. Volunteers can be effective in delivering direct services to these families. These volunteers are characterized by having gentleness, patience, empathy, and the capacity to nurture. Many have been through some very difficult experiences and can, because of their own crises, give the strength and support that others need.

Most volunteers are willing to be trained before beginning their "job." Training may involve medical, social, and legal aspects of child abuse and neglect; characteristics of the abused parent and child; and ways to motivate and encourage the parent's involvement in the treatment program.

Since caseworkers rarely have time for intensive one-on-one care and nurturing, the volunteer worker can fill the gaps, yet can be supervised and monitored by a social worker. According to authorities (Kempe and Helfer 1972), the ideal therapist is one who is prepared to become meaningfully involved in the lives of abusive parents over a period of eight to twelve months.

Some volunteer programs provide direct services to the battered child. Some are of an emergency nature, wherein their prime function is to protect the child in his home, and others are clinic- or hospital-based to provide nurturing and care outside the child's home.

One such hospital-based program is a welcome-baby program. It is designed to give support to all mothers who have just had a baby. Trained volunteers visit local hospitals twice weekly to pass out newsletters or booklets to all new moms and dads. The volunteer gives information on infant care and parenting and generally acts as an information and referral source. The material contains the volunteer's name and phone number to encourage the mother to call for further information, to request a home visit, or simply to talk.

Another hospital-based program that gives support to children who are hospitalized for a lengthy stay is called foster grandparents. This program may occur in a hospital located a great distance from the family's home. The child's family may not be able to give continuous support to their hospitalized child for a long period of time; so foster grandparents fill the gap. Many times they not only give support to the child but to the parents as well. Most states have centers for retirees who are willing to play this role because their own children and grandchildren live a distance away. Sometimes grandparents require more interaction from their families than busy families can give; so their volunteer job serves as a supplement.

In child abuse programs implemented by a state or a local public agency, such as child protective services, a volunteer component in the program is important. Most authorities agree that volunteers extend the arm of the bureaucracy and at the same time soften and humanize its operation.

Benefits accrue to both the people served and the agency. Because lay volunteers are often from the community, they also become the voice of the community and the direct link to the professionals. Volunteers often help keep programs and their organizers in touch with the community and its conscience. On the other hand, volunteers pass along to the community their understanding of the agency's functions and problems.

The volunteer's unpaid status and nonauthoritarian position within the agency allows certain types of relationships not possible for the professional caseworker. The volunteer is the one to whom the abusive parent can express fears or anger toward the agency. The volunteer can listen and act as a liaison or go-between to get action for either the client or the agency.

However, the use of volunteers is not without some problems. When the professional feels the volunteer can get results and action in a more productive way, he may feel threatened. Sometimes program professionals want to restrict volunteers to noninteraction jobs, such as providing transportation or facilitating paperwork for the family. Also, in some jobs, the professional may feel the volunteer is after his job, or that his job will be eliminated in favor of an all-volunteer staff. Finally, there may be a wide educational, social, and cultural gap; the volunteers may be better educated and in a higher socio-economic group than the staff assigned to supervise them.

Although evaluation data is difficult to obtain, almost all program organizers and staff agree that volunteers in a program contribute a unique and priceless piece to the whole child-abuse puzzle. Despite potential problems, most professionals emphasize that the programs could not continue without volunteer involvement.

Helplines

A family-crisis hotline can be a lifeline for parents who are unable to cope with stresses in their home life or in the parent-child role. It is a confidential listening-referral service, usually manned by trained volunteers. Intervention is in the form of counseling to help a person find constructive ways to cope with his problems. Ideally, the hotline provides person-to-person follow-up, which can be achieved if the hotline is located in a facility that can provide follow-up, such as a crisis center or counseling agency.

Helplines are a recent innovation, occurring all over the United States within the last decade. Since many communities have had some type of crisis hotline, they have trained their staff and lay volunteers in the basics of answering child-abuse calls.

Specifically, the caller finds a sympathetic, supportive, nonjudgmental listener and then hears of places she can go and people she can contact to get help for her problems. Sometimes a young parent needs a way to vent frustrations and built-up anger at the parenting process. She may find friends and relatives are shocked if she uses them as a sounding board. At other times a parent is ready to lash out at the child, and a brief phone conversation with a trained listener provides a cooling-off period.

Sometimes a parent, who has an unsatisfactory relationship with her child and fears she will abuse him, can find information and the proper agency or program to contact by a simple phone call. If an all-out crisis occurs, general intervention can take over, and volunteers can go to the home to rescue the child or can contact the proper agency for the help needed. Many child-abuse and neglect helplines are run directly by hospitals, voluntary crisis agencies, or protective service agencies. The twenty-four-hour helpline is an essential ingredient for many comprehensive child-abuse and treatment programs.

A *warmline* or *totline* is also a telephone answering service for parents having difficulty handling or understanding normal developmental problems of their infants, toddlers, or school children. In many programs these helplines are operated by trained volunteers or by professionals such as school psychologists, school counselors, school nurses, mental health clinic personnel, and child-development specialists. Some warmlines or totlines have volunteers who play taped messages on various requested child-development topics.

If helplines are used by abusive and neglectful parents, they can be extremely effective both in prevention and in crisis. However, getting the message out that the helpline is a free service, that it can be a child's lifesaver, and that someone wants to help parents cope is the most difficult job of the helpline staff. More community awareness of the existence of helplines, especially their nonjudgmental nature, can be an important key. However, first-hand experience by an abusive parent and then word-of-mouth explanation to others in need are the most important keys to successful usage of helplines.

6
Suggestions for Solving the Child-Abuse and Neglect Problem

The story does not end with treatment of abuse and neglect. If we concentrate only on treatment, we are taking an "after the fact" approach. If, on the other hand, we concentrate only on building awareness and designing model treatment programs, we miss the important factor of prevention—stopping abuse before it starts. If we are honest about the problem, we admit that child abuse and neglect arouse both our rage and our fear. Our rage is directed at parents who maltreat their children. Our fear is directed inward. We know that we are, at some point, capable of the same brutality. Neither of these emotions helps the child.

At present, our efforts focus more on the detection, reporting, and treatment of abuse and less on the education

156

and supportive action that prevents abuse and neglect. The state's passage of mandatory abuse-reporting laws has helped alert the public to the magnitude of the problem. The 1974 Congressional action that passed the Child Abuse Prevention and Treatment Act (PL 93-247) and established a National Center on Child Abuse and Neglect, has helped many communities establish model treatment programs. These communities need to muster enthusiasm, funds, and resource support for long-term prevention projects and programs.

More Research Needed

In order to provide a valid base for prevention programs, a greater amount of research must determine child abuse and neglect causes, characteristics, behavior patterns, emotional levels, environmental contributions, stress factors, communication difficulties, expectation differences, and a host of other data. We must know so much *more*.

Child-abuse and neglect research over the past fifteen years (the total life of almost all research on this topic) has been sketchy. Usually the number of cases studied by any one researcher is quite small. Definitions of child abuse and neglect have varied from authority to authority, and abusing families have been studied for only brief time spans.

Most concerned professionals agree that comprehensive research needs to be conducted. They suggest that larger groups of abusive families should be studied and that the studies should follow families over a number of years. Another concern is that if research is developed in conjunction with helping programs, the program model should be duplicated in other sites around the country to be sure that it really works with families living under different conditions and in different environments.

Because so many studies obtain their initial family contacts from child protective service files or law-enforcement files, the myth is perpetuated that most child abuse and neglect occurs in lower-income homes. In future studies attempts should be made to include families from all levels of society to overcome this bias. We know that abuse exists in all socioeconomic levels of society but that the wealthier class can afford to doctor-shop or move their residence if people get too intrusive.

Several specific areas of abuse are particularly underresearched. One of the areas needing more comprehensive research is the "chicken or egg" issue concerning abuse and handicapped children. Are they at higher risk for abuse and neglect because they are handicapped? Or did they become handicapped through abuse and neglect early in their lives? Which came first? The answer to these questions could help groups, agencies, and schools become more involved much earlier in possible child-abuse and neglect cases.

Another area that needs more research is the relationship between child abuse and learning disabilities, specifically central nervous-system damage. Statistics available suggest that a majority of abuse occurs before a child enters school. We know that children are tested during the first year of school and are screened and identified for special attention to meet the needs of their specific disability. But what about the abuse and neglect that occurs within the first few months of the child's life? Damage to a child's physical, mental, and emotional well-being can impede proper growth and development for four or five years until it is identified in kindergarten or grade one.

Another underresearched area is the role the child plays that might lead to abuse. Questions must be asked about the qualities in a child that might instigate or encourage a parent or caretaker's loss of control. Also related to this issue is the question of whether parent-child mismatches occur in terms of personality, behavior, and temperament. Many parents who dislike peculiarities within themselves may see these same traits in their children. The characteristic called "stubbornness" is a prime offender in this area. More research is needed to determine whether some personality characteristics are incompatible. Action could be taken to change these characteristics or to temporarily remove the child from the home or the parent from the family.

Many other areas are underresearched but probably none so much as the effect that child-development information has on parenting style and behavior. The possibility exists that early child abuse and neglect occurs because parents have expectations either too high or too low for their child. Many parents are ignorant about the particular milestones or developmental points that all children pass through. They also do not have a clear understanding that all children are unique. Although all children go through developmental milestones in the same order, some children move through them faster than others. Research to discover the basic knowledge abusive parents have compared with that of nonabusive parents might provide valuable information for preventive programs.

As more projects and programs are funded and implemented, many of these questions must be answered. The problem exists. The child being abused today will not be helped by the research conducted in the next ten years, five years, or even tomorrow.

Child Abuse and Neglect Is a Community Problem

Many people say, "I'm glad our law enforcement agencies, child protective services, and schools have a mandate to take care of the child-abuse and neglect problem, so our community doesn't have that extra burden." Although this is a common statement, the realization that those agencies and organizations *are* the community is not common. Even more difficult for community members to accept is the basic understanding that child abuse and neglect *is* a community problem. A degree of community carin gmust exist in order to support agencies in their work with the abused child and his family. Even more important, effective prevention can emerge only from a community base.

Community-developed programs usually are successful because they are based on values important to them and are designed specifically for them. Community-developed programs work because the needs that arise within the framework of those values are tailored to the geographic, cultural, and societal flavor of the members of the community.

The basic underlying values inherent in the establishment of successful community-developed child abuse and neglect programs are these (Palmer 1978):

- Belief in the human growth potential. This means that people in the community are viewed as ever-changing—not static—capable of personal growth and change.
- Rights of people to participate in decisions affecting their lives. This means that no statements of the problem, need, or solution are imposed on them but are rather developed by the community.
- Participating democracy provides the most conducive environment for human growth and development. This means shared effort offers the greatest opportunities for learning, growing, and changing.
- Social interaction increases the potential for human development. This means that when community members are exposed to many perspectives or ways of doing things, learning experience increases.
- Social interaction leads to a broadened concept of community as well as community responsibility so important to the success of child-abuse and neglect programs. This broadened community concept encourages united energies and maximized local resources.
- Every community resident and every discipline is a needed and invaluable contributor to a group process. This wedding

minimizes interdisciplinary clashes as well as cultural polarizations.

The process of community development usually works best if a facilitator within the community encourages the following flow of activity (Palmer 1978):

Facilitator—Coordinator

Group entry period—Rapport building

Needs assessment

Agencies—Enlistment of others—Civic groups

Larger nucleus formed

Selection of topic area

Consensus of commitment to that area

Study (area, people, problems, resources)

Developing action plan

Action expedition—Action evaluation

Splintering of interest groups

New action commitments

Process repetition

This flow is a productive method for basic problem-solving situations involving community-developed programs.

Out of this method the community may focus on the abusive parent's needs or on the needs of the child. Some possible community responses might be as follows:

- A "hot line" telephone system utilizing trained volunteers with medical and social support teams.
- A "crisis nursery" where children and parents may find temporary but unconditional release from interactional pressures.
- Parents' Anonymous chapters utilizing shared experiences and mutual support.
- Professional and volunteer therapy leaders and groups.
- A "shelter home" providing temporary living accommodations under the auspices of a professional, supportive staff who would be available for instruction in

home management, principles of parenting, and ways to develop positive caring relationships.

Besides these, many other community-developed projects could be successfully implemented depending on the values and need of the members of the community.

One of the most effective aspects that emerges from the community development process is the decision to form a child-abuse and neglect task force to function in the community. Specific steps toward forming such a task force make it successful. Some pitfalls, on the other hand, block forward movement. First the steps (Barry 1978):

■ *Identify the principles.* List the groups, organizations, and agencies having a mandate to report, service, or provide treatment to abused and neglected children (and families should be included). A broad representation from the community might include children's protective services, law enforcement, school personnel, doctors, clergy, and civic groups.

■ *Get a written commitment.* If the top person of the organization, group, or agency writes a letter of endorsement, that letter encourages others to volunteer their time and energy. It also encourages agency representatives to participate freely. When personnel know they are getting strong backing, they devote more time and energy to the task.

■ *Plan the first meeting.*

• *Prepare to present the facts* about child abuse and neglect. Be specific. Use local statistics. Compare them with national statistics and statistics from similar localities.

• *Prepare to build enthusiasm* for the project by explaining what other task forces have accomplished. Discuss community concern and willingness to become involved.

• *Prepare to build individual commitment* by accepting volunteered ideas and opinions. Get people personally involved.

■ *Have an agenda.*
· State the purpose of the meeting.
· Describe the task force and how it works.
· Divide into small groups. Discuss how each member perceives child abuse and neglect. Discuss needs of the community. List barriers to task force organization.
· Ask for a report from small groups. Large sheets of newsprint can be useful when small groups report back to large groups.
■ *Set priorities and define objectives.* This may not occur in the first meeting, but the small- and large-group technique may be useful here, too. Ask such questions as this: "what do you see needs to be done about child abuse and neglect in this community?" Remind groups to be realistic in setting goals. From general suggestions a list of projects will emerge. Decide on a priority ranking for each, depending on its importance and what the task force can actually accomplish.
■ *Form committees* to begin work on specific projects.
■ *Choose leadership.* List qualities desired for a leadership role. Discuss possibilities of temporary chairpersons, rotating, or cochairpersons. Choose a nominating committee to accept nominations and process applications.
■ *Decide on structure, procedure, process.* Bylaws and an organization chart may become necessary at the beginning, or later as the task force develops.
■ *Connect with the community power structure.* The task force will need all the cooperation and support it can get, and having such representatives as task force membership is one way to get cooperation. Media representation, such as newspaper, radio, and television representatives are invaluable.
■ *Get the task force in front of the public.* Presenting a "together" image to the public is important. Written goals and objectives help all members say the same thing. A public relations committee may also become the "spokesperson" for the membership.

- *Keep costs minimal.* Try to get existing agencies to absorb typing, printing, and mailing costs. Since the development of new projects will probably be an overriding goal, don't get bogged down in fund raising.
- *Provide ongoing information for membership.* Keep members current about new research, statistics, and programs on child abuse and neglect. Don't forget that hard decisions need to be made, and the general purpose of the task force group needs to be reiterated.
- *The organizer may or may not be the leader.* After choosing the leadership, encourage brainstorming solutions to problems rather than single "right" solutions. Encourage group decision making.
- *Design an evaluation process* to see if goals and objectives are achieved.

Those are the *dos,* and now here are some *don'ts* for the group's organization. Any time human nature is involved, successful relationships are unpredictable. Here are some major stumbling blocks to the task force's organization (Barry 1978):

- Don't lose sight of the abused child and his family.
- Don't get bogged down in structural procedures and organizational methods.
- Don't become a study or discussion group rather than an action group.
- Don't forget the last step: evaluation; it is important.
- Don't forget to assign committees to carry out assignments.
- Don't forget to assign reasonable deadlines for assignments or tasks to be completed.
- Don't forget to involve and advise key leaders and key agencies in the community of the task force plans, decisions, and assignments.

Community organization and development can be a moving, driving, powerful force for action. If it is used effectively and nurtured along, it can initiate invaluable projects and programs concerned with prevention, service, and treatment of child abuse and neglect.

School Personnel Are Key Detection Agents

School personnel are key figures in the prevention of child abuse and neglect. They have almost daily contact with children above the age of five. Because of the long work schedules some parents maintain, educators often have more contact hours with the child than do parents; therefore, they have the unique opportunity and responsibility to identify children in crisis and to initiate action before serious injury is inflicted.

Thirty-seven states specifically mandate that educators report suspected cases of abuse and neglect: Alabama, Alaska, Arkansas, California, Colorado, Connecticut, Delaware, Florida, Georgia, Hawaii, Idaho, Illinois, Iowa, Kansas, Kentucky, Louisiana, Maine, Massachusetts, Michigan, Minnesota, Mississippi, Missouri, Montana, Nebraska, New Mexico, New York, North Carolina, North Dakota, Ohio, Oregon, Pennsylvania, South Dakota, Virginia, Washington, West Virginia, Wisconsin, and Wyoming (Fraser 1978).

In other states, school personnel, especially teachers, counselors, secretaries, nurses, and specialists have sufficient contact with the child to identify and detect possible abuse. Certainly, skill development and training in detection awareness can make the alert and perceptive educator even more effective.

Many school districts have provided preservice or inservice days devoted to skill development and training in abuse and neglect. Unfortunately, not all districts have determined that child abuse and neglect have high priority on the list of important inservice topics. Also, smaller school districts and rural schools may have a lack of resources, both human and financial, for implementing abuse training. What administrators and planners do not realize is that volumes of free books, pamphlets, firms, and volunteer speakers can help in training teachers. It takes time and effort to coordinate these resources, but no one can argue that it is not time well spent.

The following are some topics that should be included in any training on child abuse and neglect:

- Information on how to recognize abuse and neglect.
- Presentation of the state law requiring child abuse reporting (or local school district policy if appropriate).
- Explanation of the details of reporting, such as notification of parents, school administration, law enforcement, and hospital.
- Explanation of how to write up thorough reports following a telephone report.
- Presentation of a written school policy on abuse reporting procedures. If no written school policy exists, the process of writing one may be set in motion through the training.
- Suggestions of ways to relate to and support abused children and abusive parents.
- Suggestions about how to discuss abuse and neglect situations concerning themselves and others.

Special Note: The school secretary is a key person in all parent and student contacts with the school office. It is imperative that the secretary be included in the child-abuse and neglect training. Other school staff such as food service workers, custodians, aides, and bus drivers should also be included. At times, these people have a closer one-to-one relationship with a child than teachers or other school personnel. Their observations can be invaluable.

School personnel also must know the signs concerning specific behaviors of children and attitudes of parents. Some questions they might answer are as follows:

- Is the child aggressive, disruptive, destructive, shy, withdrawn, passive, or overly compliant?

- Is the child frequently absent or late, or does he arrive early and stay late?
- Is the child inadequately dressed for the weather, unkempt, or dirty?
- Does the child appear undernourished, tired, in need of medical attention?
- Does the child have bruises, welts, and contusions? Is he frequently injured?
- Does the child complain of beatings or maltreatment?
- Are parents aggressive, highly defensive, hostile, or abusive when asked about problems concerning their child?
- Are parents apathetic or unresponsive?
- Does parental behavior appear bizarre or strange?
- Do parents show little or no concern for their child? Do they take little or no interest in their child's successes or failures? Do they act as if they do not want to be bothered about their child's school activities?
- Do the parents fail to participate in school activities or allow the child to participate?
- Do parents suddenly move to another school district or send their child to a different school when they are approached about the child's performance, behavior, or appearance?

Child-abuse workshops, seminars, presentations, symposiums, preservice and inservice programs can vary from one hour to several days or weeks, depending on how much previous training the staff has encountered. Five important points must be stressed:

- Even one hour of training in abuse and neglect awareness is better than none at all.
- *All* school personnel need to be included in the training, not just teachers.
- Abuse and neglect programs do not require a lot of resources to implement. Free and inexpensive materials and professional and volunteer lay people can be of great help.

- Although an extensive training program on child abuse and neglect may take place one year, all staff need a "reminder" at the beginning of each new school year. New staff will also need training.
- If administrators do not perceive child abuse and neglect as a priority item on school inservice programs, school personnel collectively should request such training.

Increased staff sensitivity to and awareness of the problems of child abuse will increase the likelihood that a child's and his parents' distress signals will receive intelligent and appropriate attention.

Educate Children to Protect Themselves

Abusive situations do not always occur in the home and within the family circle. Many crimes are committed by older children against younger children. Some sex offenses are committed by people who frequent schoolyards, playgrounds, and movie houses. At times the perfectly "normal, all-around" teen or preteen goes berserk and commits hideous crimes against children. As crime rates continue to increase across the country, parents, teachers, neighbors, and youth workers can help alleviate some of the child-related crimes by giving children some rules and guidelines to follow for their own protection.

Ways Children Can Protect Themselves
- Children can protect themselves by learning to be observant. Often children lapse into a dreamworld, shutting out everything and everyone. During such times, they unthinkingly step out in front of a car, run across a street against the light, or fall down and have a serious accident. Some children tend to daydream more than others, and learning observant behavior is more difficult for them. However, if they can learn to note the unusual, the suspicious, the strange behavior of others, half the battle is

won. Adults can model this behavior by commenting on unusual happenings when they are with the child. Children can learn to note descriptions of people, license plates, and vehicles or strange cars parked at the playground or schoolyard if they understand that such observation is for their own safety and well-being.

■ Children can protect themselves by never accepting gifts, candy, toys, money, or rides from strangers. They should know, beyond the shadow of a doubt, that a stranger will never be sent to pick them up from school, the store, or a movie. They should also realize that if someone calls to them from a car, they should never get close enough to be snatched or pulled into the car.

■ Children can protect themselves by admitting that a situation will never occur that will cause them to hitchhike. Hitchhiking must be a firm, unbreakable rule with no exceptions. Too often young children "pretend" to hitchhike while waiting for the bus or for a ride with their family or friends. Kidnapping, sexual abuse, or physical abuse can occur as a result of this pretend game.

■ The old-fashioned coin-loafer shoe style also had a practical purpose: if necessary, the child always had money in his shoe for a phone call. Perhaps that idea is still sound. Children can protect themselves by taping a couple of dimes into their shoes for an emergency phone call.

■ The "latch-key" child is the child who arrives home in the afternoon, several hours ahead of the rest of the family. It is not uncommon for some children to let themselves into the house, fix a snack, and either watch television or go out to play for several hours until other family members return. The child may either wear the key on his person (thus the term *latch-key*) or use a hidden key at the house or apartment. Some basic home security rules for these children are as follows:

• If the child is returning home alone, he needs to have his key in hand before he reaches the door so that he can get into the house quickly. This habit also reminds him to keep alert.
• The child should keep doors and windows locked at all times.
• No visitors should be admitted when the child's parents are not at home.
• If the phone rings, information such as "My parents aren't home," "No one is home but me," or "I'm alone" should never be given. Children can protect themselves by saying, "Mom can't come to the phone," and immediately end the conversation.

■ Older children often harass younger children for lunch or newspaper money. Young children who tend to boast about their "riches" are caught in this predicament more often than children who are quiet about their wealth. However, a child must understand that his belongings are never worth risking physical harm. This is a difficult lesson because small treasures are precious to young children.

One of the best tactics a child can use is yelling loudly to attract attention; but fighting back, running, or talking his way out of difficult situations are also useful tactics. Children should not be limited to using one tactic alone, although this depends on the child and the particular situation.

A child can learn to carry some money in a wallet or a purse and the rest in a pocket for better protection.

Self-defense techniques such as judo or karate are difficult to master and usually give a child a sense of false bravery. Although it may hurt their pride, children should know it is sometimes wiser to give in.

Ways Parents Can Help Children Protect Themselves
■ Parents can protect their children by having the kind of relationship that permits open and frank discussion of personal subjects, fears, and apprehensions. Children who say they can't talk to their parents or parents who say their

children don't listen to them are in for trouble because neither has confidence or trust in the other.

If parents find it too upsetting to talk calmly about such matters as sexual offenses, they should ask a close relative, a friend, or the child's teacher to explain appropriate safety measures.

Although it is important to talk openly and honestly about crime, parents shouldn't try to frighten a child into being careful. By their tone of voice and their body language, parents can quickly relay fears and anxieties to their children.

One important guideline to follow is never to tell children more than they can understand, especially graphic details. A measure of common sense is appropriate.

Parents should develop friendships with the parents of their children's friends. These friendships help both sets of parents keep in touch and to check on what their children are doing together.

■ Parents need to set up safety rules that have well-thought-out explanations for the whys of each rule.

• Here is one standard safety rule for most families: "I want to know where you are at all times. If you are playing in a certain area and decide to go somewhere else, let me know first." Parents often request children to call them when they arrive at their destination and when they leave for home. In this way they can monitor unusual delays and can anticipate problems that might occur. Most families set a certain time for children to come home. They ask their children to call them if they cannot meet the deadline.

• Here is another safety rule: "Tell me if you go into your friend's house to play. Call me and let me know where you are and how long you will be there." Many parents have desperately searched a neighborhood, only to find their child playing in the house next door.

• Parents may want to know the exact route their child walks to and from school so that they can pick them up if necessary. It is also important that a child walk the same way each day for safety reasons. Shortcuts through different neighborhoods with strange people or stray dogs may be dangerous for children.

• Parents have a responsibility to inform and educate their child about emergency behavior. What action to take in case of fire, accident, or another emergency is good practice for children and adults alike. A list of emergency phone numbers should be beside the phone at all times.

• Parents can model good safety behavior by taking travel precautions, such as using well-lighted traffic areas and keeping car doors locked and windows closed. In case of emergency, they should try to reach a police station or a busy, populated area. If this is not possible, they should remain in the locked car and honk the horn until help arrives. Children learn from their parents' behavior, both the good and the bad. Parents can help protect their child by modeling only the best safety behavior.

• Closely related to this point is the basic attitude parents have toward law-enforcement officers and agencies. If parents consider law-enforcement officers to be helpers— people to look to in time of emergency—children will also see them in this light. Parents should cooperate with the police and consult them immediately if any suspicious event occurs. No neighbor, relative, or friend should be shielded or protected if they harm children or commit other crimes. All obscene phone calls, exhibitionists, Peeping Toms, and "offers" should be reported immediately.

• Finally, parents should practice the "what if" game with their child. For example, "What if a stranger offers you a ride home?" "What if older children begin to hurt you to get your money?" "What if you think you are being followed?" By rehearsing some possible situations, parents can bring out their child's fears and anxieties as well as see if they know what to do in certain dangerous situations.

Ways Teachers Can Help Children Protect Themselves
■ Teachers can encourage the "buddy system." If children live near each other, teachers can help them coordinate their walk or bike route. Because "there is safety in numbers," children should be in the company of other children, older brothers and sisters, or adults, if at all possible.
■ Teachers can have children draw a map of the safest walk or bike route to school and arrange for older children to accompany younger ones.
■ Teachers can help children memorize their home phone number or the work numbers of their parents. They can also teach the child how to dial the operator or an emergency police number.
■ Teachers can offer their personal phone number as an emergency number in case the child in crisis cannot contact a parent, a neighbor or a relative.

Ways Neighbors Can Help Children Protect Themselves
One of the best preventive measures against crime is a caring neighbor. In many communities across the country, residents have volunteered to provide help for children in trouble. Sometimes these neighbors put signs in their windows to tell children where they can go if they are in trouble. Often this type of program is a deterrent against crime.

Teach a Child His Right to a Safe, Secure Environment

Children need to know they do not have to suffer abuse and neglect as a part of disciplinary measures. By the time children reach school age, they should know that whippings, beatings, bruising, burns, bites, and cuts are not the way most parents get their children to behave in acceptable ways. Perhaps open, frank discussions about disciplining methods should be held in kindergarten and first grade, wherein children will learn that since all children are different, so are all families different in their punishment of misdeeds. In some families a stern look might be all that is needed to change behavior. In other families the child might be isolated for a period of time from the rest of the family members. If there has been misuse of an item like a bicycle, perhaps it is off limits for a period of time. In still other families, a spank on the child's bottom is the last resort and the quickest and most effective method. Most families have different but appropriate methods of dealing with wrongdoings. Maltreatment, however, is never an appropriate method of changing or correcting behavior. A very fine line exists between overdisciplining and abuse, and five- and six-year-old children can learn to understand that difference.

At the same age, or at an even younger age, children can learn that no one should touch or abuse their bodies in any way. It is very hard for adults to help children learn to trust others if other adults have done bad things to them. By school age children can understand that sexual abuse is bad behavior, to be avoided at all costs. Most authorities agree that the child who has had continual sexual stimulation from adults through the early years is the most difficult to treat. Because that child seeks approval from the sexually abusive adults through coyness, teasing, and overt sexual behavior, learning appropriate methods of getting attention may be very difficult for him. Sometimes children who are used for adult sexual gratification turn to prostitution in their young adult years because of the strong impact of their early attention-getting behaviors.

Children are the greatest resource we have in our country, yet they tend to be our greatest forgotten resource at times. Before they reach school age, they may not be able to reason whether their abusive treatment is good or bad; but at school they have an opportunity to compare notes with other children their age and find out if other parents abuse or neglect their children as they are being abused and neglected. It is the responsibility of caring adults to reach out to these children and find ways to insure their right to a safe and secure environment.

Educate Preparents

If we are to reduce the number of abused and neglected children, we must look to preventive measures, beginning with today's children who are the parents of tomorrow. Educating children and teens for family life can be one of the most effective preventive measures against abuse. Comprehensive family life education should begin in kindergarten and should develop over the years through the twelfth grade. For maximum benefit, students should receive both theoretical classroom experience and practical experience, working directly with family stress, problem-solving, valuing, child development, and parenting skills. At the junior-high and high-school levels, students should have the opportunity to work directly with young children. Courses of this type should also be made available at the junior college and at college and university levels.

A course on child maltreatment should be a part of every high school's family-life curriculum. If a school district does not have a family-life curriculum, child maltreatment can become a unit in home economics, senior problems, social studies, or the humanities. Such a course of study should focus on these topics:

- Understanding nurturing and how important it is in infancy and early childhood. Understanding its relationship to the ability to achieve emotional maturity later in life.
- Comprehending how youngsters grow and develop. Understanding basic milestones and the approximate age of their achievement.
- Understanding how the use of violence in the family results in a cycle of violence as the child becomes a parent.
- Promoting an understanding of stress in personal life, in a job, in the family, and between parent and child; and helping

the child learn coping skills to manage that stress in acceptable and productive ways.

Often, high school students are not motivated to study about how children grow and develop because it is not an immediate issue in their lives. They believe parenting to be ten years in the future. However, child maltreatment is quite a different matter. Many high-school students have an interest in child abuse based on curiosity, and they later develop a deeper commitment to the study. Sometimes their interest results in a type of volunteer action to aid ongoing abuse treatment programs in the area, or they provide presentations to other groups on the problem of abuse and neglect. In some communities the organization of hotlines for abusive parents has developed out of the efforts of a group of concerned high-school students. One should never underestimate the energy, dedication, and enthusiasm of a few teenagers committed to the problem of child abuse and neglect.

All the way through school, children and youth should be working on building a positive self-image. This part of the "curriculum" is not specifically a family-life matter; it has to cut across all disciplines. The fact that a good self-concept relates very closely to success in future relationships and goal achievement should be openly and frankly discussed in many classes. Since a positive self-concept is also a strong preventive measure against child abuse and neglect in future parenting relationships, it should be consistently encouraged through the school years.

Educate Parents about Child Rearing

Since robins, rabbits, and other animals perform their parental duties without specific training, humans have assumed that "doing what comes naturally" is all that is needed to rear their young. However, in a complex world such as ours, instinct is not enough. Most human mothers and fathers need help. In fact, many young parents are almost totally unprepared for parenthood.

However, it would be naive to think that knowledge is a total solution to the problem. Even the most unskilled and the youngest of mothers often succeed blissfully, while the best educated and most intellectual do not. Sheer factual knowledge and basic parenting skills are helpful to any parent, but loving parents, a pleasant childhood, and a supportive spouse may be equally as important.

Since most parents "learn how to parent" at home as children, they usually copy methods that were used on them. Sometimes, but not usually, if they remember a painful childhood, they try to do the opposite.

Parenting is usually tied pretty closely to the type of person one is. Adults who are open, patient, warm, firm but understanding, and consistent in temperament usually provide adequate-to-good childhood experiences for their offspring. These people may even do a great job with extra guidance from books, magazine articles, and courses and classes on parenting. They care very deeply about their responsibility.

Parents who are self-centered, immature, inconsistent, easily angered or upset, fearful, and insecure, may not provide good childhood experiences for their offspring.

Can good parenting be taught? Some believe it can. Other authorities believe that parents can only learn better ways to cope with their stresses and problems related to child rearing. Either camp says that not to try to present information and education is to miss the point of the problem altogether. Many books, courses, and "packages" have been developed over the past few years for teaching good parenting skills and practices.

Some aspects have changed in the parenting arena over the last two or three decades. Unlike the large, extended families of a generation or two ago in which children grew up caring for younger children or cousins, today's small nuclear family is often isolated from relatives. Many young people grow up never having any contact with younger children, with child care, or even with baby sitting experiences. Not only is their knowledge of child development limited, but also their practical experiences and contacts with infants and toddlers is practically nil. Because of this lack of experience, most new parents have expectations of children that are often unrealistic and naive. Not knowing what to expect from a child, they punish or even physically abuse him for quite normal behavior at that stage of his development. This action may traumatize the child physically, mentally, and psychologically.

If parents seek information and education about how their child is growing and developing, they are taking the first important step toward developing good child-rearing practices. However, many parents wait until they are having problems they can't seem to solve before they reach out for help.

Volumes have been written about child growth and development, but they all seem to boil down to five major ideas or concepts. If parents fully understand these concepts and implement them, they can provide positive growth experiences and maximum learning activities for their child:
1. *The order of development is the same, but the pace of mastering that development is different for each child.* Since each child is unique, even within the same family, each reaches a milestone at a different time from another. Usually no one can speed up or slow down that development. A child will master a trick when he is ready. For example, children roll over, creep, crawl, pull themselves up, and then walk. Some children do all these activities before nine months of age; others wait until well after a year to accomplish them. Three developmental milestones often become a source of frustration to parents. Abuse or neglect may occur as a result of parents' attempts to speed up the process toward mastery of these milestones.

One of these milestones is *toilet training*. Because the success of maintaining dry diapers may be a long, slow, often messy process, many parents become impatient and resort to some sort of abuse to try to speed it up. Usually, the abuse only worsens the situation, and a vicious cycle begins to form. The child wets, abuse occurs, the child is traumatized and wets even more, the parent abuses more, and so on. If parents have had experience, have observed others, or have sought out information on toilet training, they know that infants should be started on toilet training only when they are ready. The signs of readiness are some dry diapers during the day combined with the child's awareness of being wet and communication about that wetness. Progress is usually slow until about twenty-four months when the child responds well to praise. At thirty months, urine retention lasts about five hours. By thirty-six months, the child should be well-conditioned and possibly can stay dry all night, but accidents can be expected through age five. Even between ages five and eight, wetting can occur after an especially exciting TV program, a movie, or a tiring day (O'Brien 1979). One can imagine the problems resulting if a parent says, "I was trained when I was a year old, and my kid's going to be trained by then, too!" Also, pressure can come from others in the form of a remark such as "Isn't your child trained, yet?"

A second milestone that causes problems is *self-feeding*. Children who are learning how to get food and drink into their mouths by their own efforts make terrible messes. Parents have to clean up those messes, and this can be a source of frustration to them. Often, young parents are as sensitive to the mess a child makes feeding himself as the noise a child makes when he is very hungry. One thing may lead to another, and the child is punished, sometimes severely, for a very natural part of the growth process.

A third milestone that causes trouble within the first three years of life is *thumb-sucking*. Some parents become frustrated because they see thumb-sucking as a dirty, filthy habit. Rather than ignore it, they make a big fuss, and the child wants to suck his thumb more than ever. Although the child will usually grow out of the habit if he is left alone, parents may punish him severely for continuation of this small security device. A little information and education on natural development milestones can give parents that extra bit of patience and possibly avoid an abusive situation.

2. Children need a *consistently nurtured environment* in order to feel safe and secure. If a child is loved one minute and shoved away the next, punished for a minor misbehavior and ignored for major offenses, he doesn't have a consistent, patient, caring atmosphere in which to thrive. Generally, these children become passive and unexperimentive and have several developmental lags. Routine and repetition in loving, caressing, talking, touching, playing, and generally nurturing are vital to every child's maximum growth and development. Neglect may be the result as the child fails to thrive.

3. If *positive behavior patterns* are established early in a child's life, they continue through the adolescent years when it is very important to have good communication. If parents try to respond to their child's smiles rather than cries, right at the beginning, they are rewarding the positive behavior the child is exhibiting rather than the negative behavior.

4. Parents need to understand when their child is reaching out for a piece of information or a new learning experience. That *teachable moment* is crucial in the child's overall growth and development. It may be a hug that says "Try it, you can do it," a caress, an encouragement, a smile, or a brief explanation. These moments may occur many times a day or only a few. They may be a few seconds or minutes in length. But if a parent is aware of the child's inquiry and thinking process, he can help the child take a new step forward in the growth and development process. Parents who cannot "put themselves in another's shoes," seeing through their child's eyes, can't help him in these ways. If a parent ignores this part of the child's development, it can be a form of neglect.

5. *Every child has basic rights.* One of the basic tenets of child rearing is for a parent to see his child as a unique individual quite separate from himself. Some parents who abuse their children in emotional ways see their children simply as an extension of themselves—as property to do with as they please. This attitude is still quite prevalent among many adults and is a basic reason that neighbors, friends, and relatives hesitate to become involved in child-abuse reporting. They do not want to "stick their noses in someone else's business." They must learn that when a parent is maltreating a child, that parent is violating the child's basic right to a safe and secure environment (O'Brien 1979).

Education for parenthood is a significant strategy for preventing potential child abuse and neglect. When parents are prepared for child rearing, they undertake the job with realistic expectations and with a practical knowledge that will help them deal effectively with their children.

However, some factors influencing child abuse and neglect cannot be changed by educating parents. Some of these are stresses and pressures, marital instability, fears and anxieties, and family isolation; these things weaken self-control and increase aggression. Other factors are the lack of support systems for parents and society's permissive attitude toward the use of physical force and punishment by those who care for children.

Although prevention as a strategy for dealing with child abuse and neglect needs more exploration, experimentation, and development, education for parenting is an effective way to begin to develop healthier families.

Expanded Services to
Help Parents Cope with Their Children

If we are serious about reducing child abuse and neglect in all its forms, we must advocate a more comprehensive social system that supports parents who are trying to cope with child rearing. Among the many essential ingredients of an improved social system are improved maternal and child health care, child nutrition programs, home visitor programs, homemaker services, and quality child-care facilities and staff. Expectant mothers should have the best prenatal care available. This care should consistently stress the importance of the prenatal and postnatal periods of development. Many young mothers do not have knowledge of the effects of smoking, alcohol, and other drugs on the health of their fetus or newborn.

All children must be properly *innoculated*. A greater number of states are passing child immunization laws but omit adequate means of enforcing these laws. Children are denied entrance into school without evidence of proper innoculation, but the time may be already too late in the child's life. There must be an earlier checkpoint.

It is very hard to believe, but many children in the United States and other highly developed countries are suffering from *malnutrition*. Although mothers may know what constitutes a proper diet for their children, they may have lean times or shortages when they can purchase only foods with low nutritional value. In other situations, families exist on fast foods, excluding fresh vegetables or fruits, thus existing on an imbalanced diet. Parents need more nutritional information as it relates to the use of food stamps and budgeting over a long period of time.

More programs are needed to provide *home visitors* who call on young families on their own terms. Basic information and education should be offered on the availability of prenatal and postnatal health care; child care; counseling; emergency services; immunization requirements; state, county, and city rules and regulations on licensing; employment; legal aid; and general assistance. These home visitors could also provide a consistent, caring friend for isolated families without close relatives or neighbors.

A greater number of homemaker services are needed to help keep families intact. Basic information and education in family budgeting can help reduce tensions and stresses. For example, if money is left to buy food at the end of the week, the family may survive the weekend without breakdown. If parents can sew simple clothing, cook more nutritiously and cheaply, be wiser consumers, find better housing, and understand more about how their child grows and develops, they have a better chance at survival. Home-economics information and education in the form of visiting homemakers can mean the difference between making it and not making it for borderline families.

Finally, *quality, around-the-clock child care* both in terms of staff and facilities are needed. Services such as these allow some options for working families and single parents. Many families leave very young children in the care of a slightly older child—one who himself needs adult supervision and nurturing. When sickness strikes a baby sitter, someone has to stay home with the child, or he goes unattended. Many serious accidents and illnesses have occurred because of inadequate supervision. Moreover, it is sad to see an older child saddled with responsibility beyond his age, ability, or skill level. Access to inexpensive, quality day and night care might help to alleviate some of the stress that leads to abuse and neglect.

If we really believe that children are the greatest resource we have for our future, we must support these expanded supportive family programs. The programs can help maximize the development of our resources so that they can rise to their fullest potential. This action may even have more effect on the rate of child abuse and neglect than specific programs that focus on prevention.

Summary

Some of the solutions to the child-abuse and neglect problem are more research—especially in targeted, under-researched areas—getting communities to see the abuse problem as *their* problem, assisting school personnel in their role as detection agents, informing and educating children to protect themselves, and providing information and education for preparents and parents on child-development and child-rearing services.

Ironically, as the economy becomes depressed and fewer resources are available for expanded human services, family tensions heighten, and the incidence of child abuse and neglect increases. That does not mean we give up the fight. It means we have to work harder to obtain city, state, and federal funding to assure all people a quality of life that will prevent the onset and continuation of abuse and neglect within the family unit. We must continue to work to expand the support systems for the family, so that they can make changes in employment and income levels. We must rewrite the laws so that our children—our most precious resource—will be protected, and their caretakers will be helped.

References

Barry, F. 1976. Helping families through friendship: visiting friends—emotional support for families. *A community handbook on child abuse and neglect.* Based on Family Life Developments nos. 3 and 4. Ithaca, N.Y.: Family Life Development Center, New York State College of Human Ecology, Cornell University.

Barry, F. 1978. Community task forces: getting it all together. In *Child abuse: who cares?* Human Ecology Forum, vol. 8, no. 4. Ithaca, N.Y.: New York State College of Human Ecology, Cornell University.

186

Bolton, F. G. Jr. 1975–78. Project materials: source book, basic skills manual, monographs, and specialized training manuals, Arizona Community Development for Abuse and Neglect (ACDAN), Phoenix, Arizona. Children's Bureau, U.S. Department of Health, Education, and Welfare, Grant No. 90-C-600 from National Center on Child Abuse and Neglect.

Brazelton, T. B. 1979. What it means to adopt a baby. *Redbook* (April) pp. 60–64.

Child Welfare League of America. 1974. *The neglected battered child syndrome: role reversal in parents.* New York: Child Welfare League of America.

Crawford, C. 1979. *Mommie dearest.* New York: Morrow Publishing Co.

DeLissovoy, B. 1973. Child care by adolescent parents. *Children Today* (July–August) pp. 22–25.

Donovan, D. 1978. Hey, I'm not so bad! *A community handbook on child abuse and neglect.* Ithaca, N.Y.: Family Life Development Center, New York State College of Human Ecology, Cornell University.

Dorman, R. 1979. Sexual abuse treatment programs: a search for innovation. *Family Life Developments: A resource from the Family Life Development Center* (June). Ithaca, N.Y.: Family Life Development Center, New York State College of Human Ecology, Cornell University.

Drotman, D., and Goldstein, M. S. 1977. Viewpoint: institutions are abusive. In *Institutionalized Child Abuse.* Human Ecology Forum, vol. 8, no. 1. Ithaca, N.Y.: New York State College of Human Ecology, Cornell University.

Elmer, E. 1967. *Children in jeopardy*. Pittsburgh: University of Pittsburgh Press.

Epstein, A. S. 1979. Pregnant teenagers' knowledge of infant development. Paper read at biennial meeting of the Society for Research in Child Development, 15 March 1979, San Francisco.

Fontana, V. J. 1973. *Somewhere a child is crying: maltreatment—causes and prevention*. New York: MacMillan Publishing Co.

Frazer, B. G. 1978. *The educator and child abuse*. Chicago: National Committee for the Prevention of Child Abuse.

Garbarino, J. 1977. The price of privacy in the social dynamics of child abuse. *Child Welfare*, 56:567–75.

Gil, D. G. 1970. *Violence against children: physical child abuse in the United States*. Cambridge, Mass.: Harvard University Press.

Helfer, R. 1976. Basic issues concerning prediction. In *Child abuse and neglect: the family and the community*, eds. R. E. Helfer and C. H. Kempe. Cambridge, Mass.: Ballinger Publishing Co.

Helfer, R., and Kempe, C. H. 1974. *The battered child*, 2d ed. Chicago: The University of Chicago Press.

Johnson, B., and Morse, H. 1968. Injured children and their parents. *Children* 15:147.

Kay, J. 1978. Incest: for many, its horror is a way of life. *The Arizona Daily Star*, 19 March 1978, p. 1, sec. 1, Tucson.

Kempe, C. H., and Helfer, R. 1972. *Helping the battered child and his family*. Philadelphia: Lippincott.

Kempe, R. S., and Kempe, C. H. 1978. *Child Abuse.* Cambridge, Mass.: Harvard University Press.

Kinsworthy, E. J. 1975–78. Project materials: source book. Arizona Community development for Abuse and Neglect (ACDAN), Phoenix, Arizona. Children's Bureau, U.S. Department of Health, Education, and Welfare, Grant No. 90-C-600 from National Center on Child Abuse and Neglect.

Martin, D. L. 1973. The growing horror of child abuse and the undeniable role of the schools in putting an end to it. *American School Board Journal* 160:51–55.

Martin, H. P.; Beezley, P.; Conway, E. F.; and Kempe, C. H. 1974. The development of abused children. *Advanced in Pediatrics* 21:25–73.

McCarthy, B. 1978. Child abuse in Georgia—two years experience. Paper read at 27th Annual EIS Conference, 3–7 April 1978, Atlanta, Georgia.

✕ Miller, J. K. 1976. Perspectives on child maltreatment in the military. In *Child abuse and neglect: the family and the community,* eds. R. E. Helfer and C. H. Kempe. Cambridge, Mass.: Ballinger Publishing Co.

Mnookin, R. H. 1973. Foster Care—in whose best interest? *Harvard Educational Review* 43:599–638.

National Center on Child Abuse and Neglect. 1978. *Volunteers in child abuse and neglect programs (a special report).* Children's Bureau; Administration for Children, Youth, and Families; Office of Human Development Services and Welfare, Washington, D. C.

Nation's Health. 1978. Half abuse found in poor families. *The Nation's Health* (October) p. 3.

Northern Virginia Mental Health Association. 1974. Is anybody listening? Creative approaches in the delivery of child protective services. Paper read at a public forum, 2 November 1974, Arlington.

O'Brien, S. 1979. *Cradle crier, crib courier, toddler tattler.* Newsletters for parents of newborns. Tucson: Cooperative Extension Service Publication, University of Arizona.

Osanka, F. 1979. Family violence in America. Paper read at seminar on Family Violence, 19 April 1979, at University of Arizona, Tucson.

Palmer, B. 1975–78. Project materials: Project overview. Arizona Community Development for Abuse and Neglect (ACDAN), Phoenix, Arizona. Children's Bureau, U.S. Department of Health, Education, and Welfare, Grant No. 90-C-600 from National Center on Child Abuse and Neglect.

Park, R. D., and Collmer, C. W. 1975. Child abuse: an interdisciplinary analysis. In *Review of child development research,* eds. E. Hetherington et al., vol. 5. Chicago: University of Chicago Press.

Rose, C. 1979. The legal rights of children. Paper read at Child Welfare League of America conference, 25–28 June 1979, Scottsdale, Arizona.

Roush, H. 1975–78. Project materials: basic skills manual, specialized training materials, monographs. Arizona Community Development for Abuse and Neglect (ACDAN), Phoenix, Arizona. Children's Bureau, U.S.

Department of Health, Education, and Welfare, Grant No. 90-C-600 from National Center on Child Abuse and Neglect.

Sandgrund, A.; Gaines, R. W.; and Green, A. H. 1974. Child abuse and mental retardation: a problem of cause and effect. *American Journal of Mental Deficiency* 79:327–30.

Schneider, C.; Hoffmeister, J.; and Helfer, R. 1976. A predictive screening questionnaire for potential problems in mother-child interaction. In *Child abuse and neglect: the family and the community,* eds. R. E. Helfer and C. H. Kempe. Cambridge, Mass.: Ballinger Publishing Co.

Shanas, B. 1975. Child abuse: a killer teachers can control. *Phi Delta Kappan* 56:479–82.

Soeffling, M. 1975. Abused children are exceptional children. *Exceptional Child* 42:126–33.

Steiner, H. 1975–78. Project materials: A community approach for a comprehensive coordinated system for child abuse and neglect in Arizona. Arizona Community Development for Abuse and Neglect (ACDAN), Phoenix, Arizona. Children's Bureau, U.S. Department of Health, Education, and Welfare, Grant No. 90-C-600 from National Center on Child Abuse and Neglect.

Swift, C. 1979. Testimony for U.S. House of Representatives Subcommittee on Family Violence. In *Child Abuse: who cares? Topical storms.* Human Ecology Forum, vol. 8, no. 4. Ithaca, N.Y.: New York State College on Human Ecology, Cornell University.

Titus, J. 1977. Topical storms: recommendations to end institutional child abuse. In *Institutional Child Abuse.* Human Ecology Forum, vol. 8, no. 1. Ithaca, N.Y.: New York State College of Human Ecology, Cornell University.

United States Department of Health, Education, and Welfare. 1977. *Comprehensive emergency services, a system designed to care for children in crisis.* No (OHD) 76-30099, Department of Health, Education, and Welfare, Washington, D. C.

Weisz, V. G. 1978. Preventive programs: unconstitutional viewpoint. In *Child abuse: who cares?* Human Ecology Forum, vol. 8, no. 4. Ithaca, N.Y.: New York State College of Human Ecology, Cornell University.

Wichlacz, C. R. 1975. Characteristics and management of child abuse in the U.S. Army—Europe. *Clinical Pediatrics* 14:545.

Appendix
Child Abuse Prevention
and Treatment Act
(Text of Public Law 93-247)

An Act

To provide financial assistance for a demonstration program for
the prevention, identification, and treatment of child abuse and
neglect, to establish a National Center on Child Abuse and
Neglect, and for other purposes.

Be it enacted by the Senate and House of Representatives of
the United States of America in Congress assembled, That this Act
may be cited as the "Child Abuse Prevention and Treatment Act."

The National Center on
Child Abuse

Sec. 2. (a) The Secretary of Health, Education, and Welfare
(hereinafter referred to in this Act as the "Secretary") shall

establish an office to be known as the National Center on Child Abuse and Neglect (hereinafter referred to in this Act as the "Center").

(b) The Secretary, through the Center, shall—

(1) compile, analyze, and publish a summary annually of recently conducted and currently conducted research on child abuse and neglect;

(2) develop and maintain an information clearinghouse on all programs, including private programs, showing promise of success, for the prevention, identification, and treatment of child abuse and neglect;

(3) compile and publish training materials for personnel who are engaged or intend to engage in the prevention, identification, and treatment of child abuse and neglect;

(4) provide technical assistance (directly or through grant or contract) to public and nonprofit private agencies and organizations to assist them in planning, improving, developing, and carrying out programs and activities relating to the prevention, identification, and treatment of child abuse and neglect;

(5) conduct research into the causes of child abuse and neglect and into the prevention, identification, and treatment thereof; and

(6) make a complete and full study and investigation of the national incidence of child abuse and neglect, including a determination of the extent to which incidents of child abuse and neglect are increasing in number or severity.

Definition

Sec. 3. For purposes of this Act the term "child abuse and neglect" means the physical or mental injury, sexual abuse, negligent treatment, or maltreatment of a child under the age of eighteen by a person who is responsible for the child's welfare under circumstances which indicate that the child's health or welfare is harmed or threatened thereby, as determined in accordance with regulations prescribed by the Secretary.

Demonstration Programs and Projects

Sec. 4. (a) The Secretary, through the Center, is authorized to make grants to, and enter into contracts with, public agencies or

nonprofit private organizations (or combinations thereof) for
demonstration programs and projects designed to prevent, identify,
and treat child abuse and neglect. Grants or contracts under this
subsection may be—

> (1) for the development and establishment of training
> programs for professional and paraprofessional personnel
> in the field of medicine, law, education, social work, and
> other relevant fields who are engaged in, or intend to work
> in, the field of prevention, identification, and treatment of
> child abuse and neglect; and training programs for
> children, and for persons responsible for the welfare of
> children, in methods of protecting children from child
> abuse and neglect;
>
> (2) for the establishment and maintenance of centers,
> serving defined geographic areas, staffed by
> multidisciplinary teams of personnel trained in the
> prevention, identification, and treatment of child abuse
> and neglect cases, to provide a broad range of services
> related to child abuse and neglect, including direct
> support and supervision of satellite centers and attention
> homes, as well as providing advice and consultation to
> individuals, agencies, and organizations which request such
> services;
>
> (3) for furnishing services of teams of professional and
> paraprofessional personnel who are trained in the
> prevention, identification, and treatment of child abuse
> and neglect cases, on a consulting basis to small
> communities where such services are not available; and
>
> (4) for such other innovative programs and projects,
> including programs and projects for parent self-help, and
> for prevention and treatment of drug-related child abuse
> and neglect, that show promise of successfully preventing
> or treating cases of child abuse and neglect as the
> Secretary may approve.

Not less than 50 per centum of the funds appropriate under this
Act for any fiscal year shall be used only for carrying out the
provisions of this subsection.

> (b) (1) Of the sums appropriated under this Act for any fiscal
> year, not less than 5 per centum and not more than 20 per
> centum may be used by the Secretary for making grants to the
> States for the payment of reasonable and necessary expenses
> for the purpose of assisting the States in developing,

strengthening, and carrying out child abuse and neglect prevention and treatment programs.

(2) In order for a State to qualify for assistance under this subsection, such State shall—

(A) have in effect a State child abuse and neglect law which shall include provisions for immunity for persons reporting instances of child abuse and neglect from prosecution, under any State or local law, arising out of such reporting;

(B) provide for the reporting of known and suspected instances of child abuse and neglect;

(C) provide that upon receipt of a report of known or suspected instances of child abuse or neglect an investigation shall be initiated promptly to substantiate the accuracy of the report, and, upon a finding of abuse or neglect, immediate steps shall be taken to protect the health and welfare of the abused or neglected child, as well as that of any other child under the same care who may be in danger of abuse or neglect;

(D) demonstrate that there are in effect throughout the State, in connection with the enforcement of child abuse and neglect laws and with the reporting of suspected instances of child abuse and neglect, such administrative procedures, such personnel trained in child abuse and neglect prevention and treatment, such training procedures, such institutional and other facilities (public and private), and such related multidisciplinary programs and services as may be necessary or appropriate to assure that the State will deal effectively with child abuse and neglect cases in the State;

(E) provide for methods to preserve the confidentiality of all records in order to protect the rights of the child, his parents or guardians;

(F) provide for the cooperation of law enforcement officials, courts of competent jurisdiction, and appropriate State agencies providing human services;

(G) provide that in every case involving an abused or neglected child which results in a judicial proceeding a guardian ad litem shall be appointed to represent the child in such proceedings;

(H) provide that the aggregate of support for programs or projects related to child abuse and neglect assisted by State funds shall not be reduced below the level provided during fiscal year 1973, and set forth policies and procedures designed to assure that Federal funds made available under this Act for any fiscal year will be so used to supplement and, to the extent practicable, increase the level of State funds which would, in the absence of Federal funds, be available for such programs and projects;

(I) provide for dissemination of information to the general public with respect to the problem of child abuse and neglect and the facilities and prevention and treatment methods available to combat instances of child abuse and neglect; and

(J) to the extent feasible, insure that parental organizations combating child abuse and neglect receive preferential treatment.

(3) Programs or projects related to child abuse and neglect assisted under part A or B of title IV of the Social Security Act shall comply with the requirements set forth in clauses (B), (C), (E), and (F) of paragraph (2).

(c) Assistance provided pursuant to this section shall not be available for construction of facilities; however, the Secretary is authorized to supply such assistance for the lease or rental of facilities where adequate facilities are not otherwise available, and for repair or minor remodeling or alteration of existing facilities.

(d) The Secretary shall establish criteria designed to achieve equitable distribution of assistance under this section among the States, among geographic areas of the Nation, and among rural and urban areas. To the extent possible, citizens of each State shall receive assistance from at least one project under this section.

Authorization

Sec. 5. There are hereby authorized to be appropriated for the purposes of this Act $15,000,000 for the fiscal year ending June 30, 1974, $20,000,000 for the fiscal year ending June 30, 1975, and $25,000,000 for the fiscal year ending June 30, 1976, and for the succeeding fiscal year.

Advisory Board on Child
Abuse and Neglect

Sec. 6. (a) The Secretary shall, within sixty days after the date of enactment of this Act, appoint an Advisory Board on Child Abuse and Neglect (hereinafter referred to as the "Advisory Board"), which shall be composed of representatives from Federal agencies with responsibility for programs and activities related to child abuse and neglect, including the Office of Child Development, the Office of Education, the National Institute of Education, the National Institute of Mental Health, the National Institute of Child Health ahd Human Development, the Social and Rehabilitation Service, and the Health Services Administration. The Advisory Board shall assist the Secretary in coordinating programs and activities related to child abuse and neglect administered or assisted under this Act with such programs and activities administered or assisted by the Federal agencies whose representatives are members of the Advisory Board. The Advisory Board shall also assist the Secretary in the development of Federal standards for child abuse and neglect prevention and treatment programs and projects.

(b) The Advisory Board shall prepare and submit, within eighteen months after the date of enactment of this Act, to the President and to the Congress a report on the programs assisted under this Act and the programs, projects, and activities related to child abuse and neglect administered or assisted by the Federal agencies whose representatives are members of the Advisory Board. Such report shall include a study of the relationship between drug addiction and child abuse and neglect.

(c) Of the funds appropriate under section 5, one-half of 1 per centum, or $1,000,000, whichever is the lesser, may be used by the Secretary only for purposes of the report under subsection (b).

Coordination

Sec. 7. The Secretary shall promulgate regulations and make such arrangements as may be necessary or appropriate to ensure that there is effective coordination between programs related to child abuse and neglect under this Act and other such programs which are assisted by Federal funds.

Approved January 31, 1974.